THE LONG JOURNEY HOME

The Road to Forgiveness
7 Steps to Consciousness:
A Blueprint for Divine Potential

SHEILA GAUTREAUX

BALBOA.
PRESS

A DIVISION OF HAY HOUSE

Balboa Press books may be ordered through booksellers or by contacting:

Balboa Press
A Division of Hay House
1663 Liberty Drive
Bloomington, IN 47403
www.balboapress.com
1 (877) 407-4847

Because of the dynamic nature of the Internet, any web addresses or links contained in this book may have changed since publication and may no longer be valid. The views expressed in this work are solely those of the author and do not necessarily reflect the views of the publisher, and the publisher hereby disclaims any responsibility for them.

The author of this book does not dispense medical advice or prescribe the use of any technique as a form of treatment for physical, emotional, or medical problems without the advice of a physician, either directly or indirectly. The intent of the author is only to offer information of a general nature to help you in your quest for emotional and spiritual well-being. In the event you use any of the information in this book for yourself, which is your constitutional right, the author and the publisher assume no responsibility for your actions.

Any people depicted in stock imagery provided by Thinkstock are models, and such images are being used for illustrative purposes only. Certain stock imagery © Thinkstock.

Print information available on the last page.

ISBN: 978-1-5043-6870-4 (sc)
ISBN: 978-1-5043-6879-7 (e)

Library of Congress Control Number: 2016917762

Balboa Press rev. date: 11/07/2016

The ocean roared
The wind danced through my locks
And the setting sun
Crafted artistic patterns
Across the cloud draped sky
From somewhere down deep
I prayed a prayer
God help me get back
To the place I came from.

Sheila Gautreaux
November 11, 2015
Asilomar Conference Grounds
Pacific Grove, CA

ACKNOWLEDGEMENTS

God is the Guiding Force in front of and behind everything I am and do.

My Children, Family and Friends are always an inspiration in my life and so, too, the inspiration for everything I write, speak and teach; however, so are those who come and push my buttons to make me a better person.

My dear friend, Cindy Farris, is the one who made it possible for this book to be completed and worked tirelessly day and night to do so.

If Robert Brumet, one of my favorite instructors at Unity Institute, hadn't written "This should be a book," this wouldn't be a book.

FOREWORD

It is always my great joy to edit one of Sheila's books. My first editing experience with her was through the second edition of *Praying Through a Storm*. I happened to be in the midst of the storm of my Dad's illness as I was editing. Reading through the book and the prayers over and over saw me through a most difficult time.

I once again find myself in a place where what Sheila is putting to paper (okay, computer) resonates deep within my soul. While she speaks of her journey and the journey of her daughter Sian, she also speaks of my journey through life, through spiritual growth, through forgiveness and into the next phase of my life's purpose… whatever Spirit has in store for me!

If you allow yourself to become immersed in the reading, the exercises, and the energy of this book, you will find that "inexplicable" things will happen for you. Certain passages, I believe, were written for my eyes only – except Sheila is sharing them with you. Other passages were answers to prayers, guideposts that I'm doing my work and reminders of WHOSE I AM!

As you read, see if you do not resonate with the words, thoughts and feelings written. See if the concepts presented here can be immediately absorbed into your present consciousness and move you into a more peaceful state. And notice; if you are willing – or

even willing to be willing – how this may also be your journey…
it certainly has been mine!

May you always be blessed…

Rev. Cindy Farris, LUT

PREFACE

In the year 2000, or 2001 if we lean more toward being scientifically precise, we reached this New Millennium. The catastrophic occurrences that were predicted and expected on the first day of the calendar year, based on prophecies of ancient cultures, did not happen.

Or did they?

Though the world did not end in the wake of a collision of the planets, the sun did not descend and burn the planet to its core and the nervous finger poised above the nuclear trigger did not press it, the world *has* ended—at least the world as we knew it. There has been an unquestionable shift in consciousness that continues at an accelerated pace, which makes it essential for humankind to live and co-create from a new awareness.

More and more sleeping souls are awakening from their illusory dream that this is it. People are discovering that their lives are fragmentary and empty of true meaning. The youth of the world are rebelling and are no longer interested in accepting this divine madness merely because to expect otherwise is pointless. The current socio-economic and political process is making a desperate last-gasp effort to survive. The world is screaming: "We're mad as hell and we're not going to take it anymore!"[1]

The energy of fear has taken a front-row seat in our psyche and

---

[1] *Network,* Sydney Lumet, MGM/UA, 1976.

is playing itself out on the big screen of our lives in a Technicolor display of war, poverty, homelessness, disease and violence. We are feeling lost, alone, and afraid that we are hanging out here all by ourselves.

Now more than ever there is a need to provide something sustaining to fill the void left by our meaningless pursuits for bigger, better, greater and more. But what?

This book utilizes the odyssey of *The Prodigal Son* and the process of Forgiveness to demonstrate the break in our connection with God, resulting from an erroneous belief system about who we are, our purpose for this spiritual journey on a human plane and the way back to a home we never left.

Included are prayers, meditations, affirmations and exercises to strengthen the concepts set forth by the book and provide guideposts along our journey home.

The book actually began with a paper[2] written for a class I took with Rev. Robert Brumet at Unity Village, while studying to become a Licensed Unity Teacher. In 1999 I created a workshop as a vehicle for presenting the concepts of Conscious Evolution in a more digestible manner. Both have laid the foundation for *The Long Journey Home.* Since then I have grown in leaps and bounds, delving more deeply into Quantum Mechanics, leading Course in Miracles groups year after year, finding my passion through the work of Colin Tipping's *Radical Forgiveness* and experiencing the abrupt and unexpected dissolution of my marriage. My journey, both joyous and painful, has inexplicably led me away from a book I was previously writing. The original concept of this book required I answer a new call to reshape the direction I was going and bring it home along a completely new path. Perhaps, its ultimate purpose was to lead me to the new path that would bring me home.

---

[2] CONSCIOUS EVOLUTION: A Blue Print for Divine Potential and Reintegration of the Collective, Sheila Gautreaux, 1999.

And what better time than this to do so, when the evidence of a planetary shift is right before us! The emergence of a new world order is apparent as we witness the collapse of an ego-based financial system and the rise of evolutionary revolution or revolutionary evolution. We are also witness to an increase in compassion and we-centered humanitarianism as more people reach out to those in need within their local and global communities. In the unfolding of a diverse egalitarian political process we saw a woman and an African-American simultaneously seeking election as president of the United States—ultimately, electing our first African-American to the highest office in our nation.

Although many would believe this shift has created further division, I believe it has given us the courage to wake up, speak out and take back the control of our lives from outer circumstances and other people to whom we gave it.

The Long Journey Home is about our journey from the break with the host body through the bewildering struggle to discover who we are, why we are here and, ultimately, to our return home, and is everyone's story regardless of religion, theology or politics. Whether we believe in evolutionism or creationism or both of them, when viewed metaphysically, both represent our *Long Journey Home.*

Perhaps you are able to relate personally with the journey of the Prodigal Son; however, whether or not that is the case, this book may provide insights and valuable tools to review your own journey and make a course correction if necessary.

I hope you enjoy reading this book as much as I have enjoyed having it written through me. Sit back. Relax. Enjoy the ride!

Sheila

INTRODUCTION

In the United States alone, according to runawayswitchboard.org, there are 1.3 million homeless youth on the streets. The data is difficult to collect due to differences in reporting between agencies. However, between 2003 and 2008, it was reported there was a 200% increase in homeless youth on the streets.

What causes us to leave home? With the exception of those persons living under deplorable, abusive or life-threatening conditions, what compels us to leave the familiar warmth, comfort and safety of home and family for the unknown?

Several websites devoted to creating awareness of this growing problem and supporting runaway teens tell us that 47% report conflict with a parent or guardian as the reason for leaving home.

The most famous runaway of all times is the fictional character in the bible known only as "The Prodigal Son" who left a life of wealth and privilege for the adventure of the open road. After blowing all the money from the inheritance he had demanded from his father, he found himself homeless, experiencing pain and suffering and wishing he could eat as well as the pigs he fed to make money.

What was he thinking?

To give him credit the Prodigal Son did come to his senses and made his way back home where, much to his shock and gratitude, he was welcomed with open arms and allowed to return to the fold. He was forgiven.

But what urges drove him to make this journey in the first place?

He wanted to find himself, to discover his individuality and test the limits of his ability to survive outside of the confines of family and home. In other words, he wanted to prove he could do it.

In a way, this is our story; this is the story of all humans when as souls we leave the comfort and safety of the Unmanifest Realm—referred to as Heaven, the Allness or Nirvana by various traditions—and set out on this journey called humanity in this place called Earth or the Manifest Realm of existence. Sometimes we, too, find ourselves living in fear and pain and suffering and must come to ourselves (our senses) and find our way back to the realization of who we are and whose we are.

Why would we want to make this journey? Since we are, what can we learn from the Prodigal Son? What is home and how do we get back there? After putting forth so much effort to leave why do we then work so hard to get back there?

The dictionary defines *home* as *a place where a person, family or household lives together;* however, when I think of the word *home* it always takes me back to one of my all-time favorite musicals, *The Wiz*. The main character, Dorothy, who is desperately attempting to get back home to Kansas, sings of her longing by describing what home is for her:

> *When I think of home, I think of a place where there is love overflowing. I wish I was there. I wish I was back there, to a place I've been knowing...* [3]

---

[3] Smalls, Charlie, *The Wiz*, "Home", 1974.

From Dorothy's perspective, home is a place of love—constant, continuous and "overflowing." In her song is the evident longing to get back to a place where she has known a love like no other. Obviously, she is comparing it to what she has been experiencing along the way of that strange journey on which she found herself.

Could our reflections and memories of *home* be similar to Dorothy's? What brought us to this strange journey called the Human Experience? If it was so wonderful, why did we leave home in the first place?

In Dorothy's case, it was a tornado that tossed her into the illusion of having left home. In our case it was a "forgetting" that tossed us into the illusion of separation from our Creator—our home—and sent us spiraling into a whirlwind of pain and suffering, chaos and confusion.

In Dorothy's experience, she connected with a strange cast and crew of fellow travelers along her journey home who taught her many things about herself, helped her find her way to the Wizard and, ultimately, home. She had to discover that she had always had all that she needed within her to get home. It was a journey of self-discovery.

Interestingly, as she helped the Scarecrow, the Tin Man and the Cowardly Lion find their intelligence, heart and courage, her own was awakened. As Radical Forgiveness points out: "If you spot it, you got it!" What we see in others is merely a reflection of what is within us. As Dorothy saw the power in her new friends, her own power was awakened.

In our case, we daily connect with all of the characters in the drama we have created to support us in discovering who we are and help us find our way to our Wizard, our Divinity. Our work is to discover that the power to go home is and has always been within us the whole time.

Unlike Dorothy, we left home to experience ourselves as the

light in the midst of our illusion of darkness. You might say that we are the Prodigal Children. Like the *Prodigal Son* of the Bible, we were not content to be in a heavenly state as spiritual beings; we wanted to *experience* ourselves as spiritual beings and in order to do that we had to experience the opposite of what we *knew* ourselves to be—we had to discover our true nature as we journeyed through pain and suffering.

To efficiently facilitate this learning experience, it was necessary to have what Colin Tipping calls *spiritual amnesia*[4] to make the experience more real—what *A Course in Miracles* calls the *forgetting*. If, as Souls on this journey of experiences for the purpose of growth or evolution, we knew what was going on there would be no real experience. It is the emotional impact of these spiritual lessons that provides the greatest opportunity for growth and evolution.

In *Teach Us To Pray*, Charles and Cora Fillmore tell us:

> *What we all need is a better understanding of the principles at the very foundation of Being, of the spiritual character of God, and especially of the omnipresence of the spiritual principles. Then we need to understand our relation to these spiritual principles and what we have to do to make them operative in our mind and affairs*[5].

Colin Tipping says, "We are not the victims of random acts of being in the right place at the right time or the wrong place at the wrong time or having good or bad luck; our lives are purposeful and have meaning."[6] If this is true, then everything we encounter

---

[4] *Radical Forgiveness*, Colin Tipping, 13 Global Publications, 1997.
[5] *Teach Us To Pray*, Charles and Cora Fillmore, Unity Classic Library, 1941, page 159.
[6] *Radical Forgiveness*, Colin Tipping, 13 Global Publications, 1997.

along this journey is pointing to a meaningful outcome. This must, then, give us some degree of comfort and may be the very impetus that inspires us to return home.

According to policemag.com, when it comes to runaways returning home:

> *About 20 percent of juveniles return home within the first 24 hours and 75 percent are home within a week. More determined runaways may engage in "couch surfing," staying with a number of different acquaintances for short periods of time. When these resources are exhausted, they usually head home or have no alternative but to head to the streets. Less than one percent of juvenile runaways never return home[7].*

So we do return home; however, the journey is often fraught with challenges, stumbling blocks, uncertainty and frequently a great degree of pain and suffering. As we know from Dorothy's attempts to get back to Kansas and as we will see from the experience of *The Prodigal Son* as he makes his Long Journey Home, both have similar experiences.

What is the journey? Why is it so long?

The *Journey* is the sum total of the experiences and processes of learning and growing we encounter as we step away from home through finding our way back. It is what changes us—what creates transformation and a shift in consciousness. It is not the walk *in* the "valley of the shadow of death" that makes a difference; it is what we discover as we walk *through* the "valley."

The journey is long because we struggle against it in our efforts to have it our way, as if our way has worked for us before. We resist the natural movement orchestrated by our Spiritual Intelligence,

---

[7] www.policemag.com

as Colin Tipping calls our inner guide in his Radical Forgiveness process, and we continually find ourselves digging our way out of the hole we keep falling into. When we surrender, as you will see in the case of the Prodigal Son, we are effortlessly led to our destination—to *Home*.

So how do we get back?

There is much we can learn from the journey of the *Prodigal Son* and we will use all of his experiences, choices, challenges and discoveries to support us in finding our own way *Home*.

THE PARABLE OF THE PRODIGAL SON

¹¹Then Jesus said, "There was a man who had two sons. ¹²The younger of them said to his father, 'Father, give me the share of the property that will belong to me.' So he divided his property between them. ¹³A few days later the younger son gathered all he had and traveled to a distant country, and there he squandered his property in dissolute living. ¹⁴When he had spent everything, a severe famine took place throughout that country, and he began to be in need. ¹⁵So he went and hired himself out to one of the citizens of that country, who sent him to his fields to feed the pigs. ¹⁶He would gladly have filled himself with the pods that the pigs were eating; and no one gave him anything. ¹⁷But when he came to himself he said, 'How many of my father's hired hands have bread enough and to spare, but here I am dying of hunger! ¹⁸I will get up and go to my father, and I will say to him, "Father, I have sinned against heaven and before you; ¹⁹I am no longer worthy to be called your son; treat me like one of your hired hands."' ²⁰So he set off and went to his father. But while he was still far off, his father saw him and was filled with compassion; he ran and put his arms around him and kissed him. ²¹Then the son said to him, 'Father, I have sinned against heaven and before you; I am no longer worthy to be called your son.' ²²But the father said to his slaves, 'Quickly, bring out a robe—the best one—and put it on

him; put a ring on his finger and sandals on his feet. [23]And get the fatted calf and kill it, and let us eat and celebrate; [24]for this son of mine was dead and is alive again; he was lost and is found!' And they began to celebrate.

[25]"Now his elder son was in the field; and when he came and approached the house, he heard music and dancing. [26]He called one of the slaves and asked what was going on. [27]He replied, 'Your brother has come, and your father has killed the fatted calf, because he has got him back safe and sound.' [28]Then he became angry and refused to go in. His father came out and began to plead with him. [29]But he answered his father, 'Listen! For all these years I have been working like a slave for you, and I have never disobeyed your command; yet you have never given me even a young goat so that I might celebrate with my friends.' [30]But when this son of yours came back, who has devoured your property with prostitutes; you killed the fatted calf for him. [31]Then the father said to him, 'Son, you are always with me, and all that is mine is yours. [32]But we had to celebrate and rejoice, because this brother of yours was dead and has come to life; he was lost and has been found.'" ~ Lk 15:11-32 NRSV

I

DISCOVERING OUR PLACE
IN THE COSMOS

STEP ONE — Who am I?

[11]Then Jesus said, "There was a certain man who had two sons. [12]The younger of them said to his father, 'Father, give me the share of property that will belong to me.' So he divided his property between."
~ Luke 15:11-12

Whether you are Christian, Jew, Muslim, Buddhist, Hindu, or align with any other religious tradition, a compilation thereof or none at all, you have more than likely heard of the parable of *The Prodigal Son.* The great spiritual teacher and way-shower of Christian theology, Jesus the Christ, used parables as a teaching modality to bring home a truth principle he was attempting to impress upon the minds of those who came to hear his profound wisdom.

The word *parable* comes from the Latin word *parabola,* which simply means to compare two things. An analogy is made between something you are familiar with in order to help you understand something that is new to you. It is a short allegorical story designed to convey some truth, religious principle or moral lesson. Charles

Fillmore, co-founder of Unity, called it an "earthly story with a heavenly meaning." In other words, it is an everyday example of a life experience that teaches us something about the deeper place of awareness and wisdom within us.

Jesus frequently took everyday incidents from people's lives to demonstrate a spiritual truth. He artfully utilized this method to speak to people right where they were in intellect, understanding and consciousness. They could take the story home with them and use it on Monday morning when life began to happen to them.

As discussed in the Introduction, this can also be referred to as a Teach-Point that inspires Student Engagement. If the student gets it, the student will become engaged in using it to transform their own life and, eventually, teach it to others.

The Parable of the *Prodigal Son* is probably one of the most widely quoted, taught, preached and interpreted passage in churches around the world. It is found in the New Testament book of Luke, Chapter 15, and Verses 11-32. You may read it in its complete form in the preface; however, here I will give you a synopsis of the story since we will be using each of the verses throughout the book.

A wealthy man had two sons, one of whom was a very hard worker—devoted, dedicated and committed to helping his father with the family business—but the other son wanted to go out and experience life—to be adventurous, to "find" himself. The latter son requested his portion of the inheritance in advance. He wasn't willing to wait until his father died. He wanted it right then so he could enjoy it before he got too old. (Well, that's my take on it anyway.) His father acquiesced and gave him the money, with which he immediately went to another land, partied, spent recklessly and soon used it all up. While he had it, he had many friends to help him spend it but after it was gone, all of his friends were gone too. (God Bless the Child who's got his own.)

He found himself homeless, working for someone who gave him a job feeding pigs, and he was longing to eat from the food he fed to the pigs. It was at this moment that scripture says: "he came to himself" (woke up) and realized what he had left behind—what he had given up—thinking there was something better "out there." He decided to go home. When he got there he humbly apologized to his father and simply asked to be hired as one of the servants because he no longer deserved to be called his son. The father welcomed him home like royalty, had a feast prepared, put a beautiful robe on him, new sandals on his feet, and a ring on his finger.

And the other brother? He was angry that his younger brother had foolishly thrown away his inheritance and left all the work to him and was now returning home and being treated like royalty or, in modern terms, a "Rock Star". His father reminded him that, although he had been there with him all the time and he appreciated this, they should rejoice because his brother had been "dead but was now alive again, was lost but now was found."

The journey of the *Prodigal Son* was a spiritual path that led him away from home, through the challenges of the world of duality and back again to his home as a beloved son who would always be welcomed home. It was a journey of finding himself through the experience of pain and suffering, and coming to the realization that "out there" was not all that it was cracked up to be—in here is the only real place there is.

The *Prodigal Son* was living the good and perfect life with the Father, but he was not yet aware of his true identity as the child of a loving Father whose good pleasure was to freely give him everything he could ever possibly wish for. He was not yet cognizant of his spiritual identity; his connection to his Father, his brother and everything else. He was unaware that he was an important piece of the puzzle and that every other piece of the puzzle was important to him.

In the *Revealing Word*, it says:

> *The "two sons" of Luke 15:11 are the two departments of the soul, or consciousness. The son who stayed at home is the religious or moral nature; the son who went into the far country is the human phase of the soul, in which are the appetites and passions*[8].

We might say the *Prodigal Son* represents the Ego.

When we are immature, we do not recognize who we are and whose we are. We believe we are separate and apart from Spirit and from all creation, causing us to feel a void or emptiness within, which drives us to fill it with things—to go seeking for that which we believe we are lacking.

Metaphysically, the *Prodigal Son* represents that immature aspect of us that is not fully aware of its spiritual nature and believes that material substance is the key to happiness and comes from sources outside of us; i.e., jobs, paychecks, Stock Market, SSI, 401k, etc. Our focus becomes acquiring more of this substance out of fear that there is not enough to go around. We then move ourselves further away from our true Source into a consciousness of materiality and the senses by seeking better jobs, higher salaries and bigger investments. Fearing lack, we become desperate; we do not recognize who we are and whose we are. We believe we are separate and apart from Spirit and from all creation, causing us to feel a void or emptiness within, which drives us to fill it with things—to go seeking for that which we believe we are lacking.

The Prodigal Son saw his Father as someone who had "his" and was powerful, important and highly regarded. He thought that,

---

[8] *Revealing Word,* Charles Fillmore, Unity School of Christianity, 1959, page 181.

by having his own, he would feel a sense of power, not realizing that his power was within him. He decided to take his portion of the inheritance and go out into the world of humanity to build his own power base. His was a two-fold journey of *involution* and *evolution*.

Involution

"Involution (infolding); always precedes evolution (unfolding); that which is involved in mind evolves through matter."[9]

All of God's works are created first in Mind as perfect ideas; God creates the ideas that form the things. This is involution.[10]

Spirit gets lost in its own creation—moving from God—a forgetting[11].

Involution is the starting point of every idea and carries the potential for evolution.

The idea to leave home—his father's house—began within the mind of this young man and was the starting point of his journey to return home after having experiences that sparked a process of evolution that inspired an awakened consciousness.

---

[9] *The Revealing Word*, Charles Fillmore, Unity School of Christianity, 1959, page 109.

[10] *Dynamics for Living*, Charles Fillmore, Unity School of Christianity, 1997.

[11] "Conscious Evolution Course", Rev. Robert Brumet (theologian/instructor), Unity Village, 1998.

Evolution

"The development achieved by man working under spiritual law... the unfolding in consciousness of that which God involved in man in the beginning." "Spiritual evolution is the unfolding of the Spirit of God into expression.[12]

Ideas are made into form and shape. The working out in manifestation of what Mind has involved. Whatever Mind commends to be brought forth will be brought forth by and through the law of evolution inherent in Being.[13]

Unfolding of Potential; unfolding of Spirit back into itself; moving to God – a remembering.[14]

Evolution is the outward expression or manifestation of the idea.

In philosophical and metaphysical concepts about *Spiritual Evolution,* the Involution/Evolution Arc is diagrammed as a "circle" and is described as a process by which Spirit descends into humans and then ascends back to Spirit. This concept beautifully implies the nature of the journey of *The Prodigal Son.* At the point of his idea to leave home, Spirit prompts his awakening and the culmination of his journey is the ascending back to Spirit.

---

[12] *The Revealing Word*, Charles Fillmore, Unity School of Christianity, 1959, page 65
[13] *Dynamics for Living*, Charles Fillmore, Unity, 1997.
[14]

"Conscious Evolution Course", Rev. Robert Brumet, Unity Village, 1998.

The journey itself, with its ups and downs, excitement and disappointment, success and failure, was the out-picturing or expression of the idea to leave home in his unconscious state and contained all of the elements necessary for the son's evolution in consciousness.

As spiritual beings having a spiritual experience on a human plane in a body, we are evolving through the processes of our lives as an expression of the idea that was involved in mind to discover who we were on our way back home.

Understanding the concepts of *involution* and *evolution* makes a clear case for the teachings by many great Masters that every idea comes pre-packaged with a perfect plan for fulfillment; therefore, in the case of the Prodigal Son, the ultimate purpose of his journey was to return home.

---

[15] http://www.kheper.net

The traditional theological approach perceives the *Prodigal Son* as representing a "fall from Grace;" however, if we look deeper, we might glimpse an analogy of our own journey of conscious evolution or a collective movement toward awakening.

At each stage of biological evolution, from subatomic particles to atoms to molecules to mega-molecules to cells to simple forms of life to human, the forms begin to reproduce and struggle for space. The critical mass occurs and a new stage of evolution happens.

Similarly, within each stage of our evolution in consciousness from mere existence and curiosity to complex thought processes, the brain (or mind) must expand to accommodate the increasing amounts of information streaming in as we discover more about ourselves. The Quantum Scientists say that the more we seek to know about the universe, the larger and more complex it becomes.

If this is true, then the journey of the *Prodigal Son* was not only pre-wired from birth but was a necessary experience for his evolution in consciousness.

Spirit exists within each phase of the process, whether we are aware of it or not. We do not grow *to* the next stage of evolution; we grow *through* the next stage. So the Prodigal Son was experiencing a growth process through his next stage in evolution.

Todd Michael tells us in *The Hidden Parables* that:

> *"If the parables are all about you, and what happens inside you as you progress along the path, then the prodigal son is obviously the thought form that strays from the center. It is the wave form propagating itself outward. Such a decentralizing idea or sensory impression quickly takes on the convincing illusion of a separate conscious event and we become lost in it."*[16]

---

[16] *The Hidden Parables: Activating the Secrets of the Gospels,* Todd Michael, 2008.

Michael is saying that there "never was a separation or leaving home" but merely the natural "upwardly progressive movement of Spirit"[17] as it evolves toward greater expression in us, in our lives and in the universe. What appears to be *separation* is a *forgetting* as Brumet puts it. We simply forgot the original purpose and direction of our mission.

Another significant thing about both cellular evolution and conscious evolution is that prior to moving from one stage to another, there is a shake-up before there is activity. This occurs as a newly rising entity, concept or belief system, meets up with an old one. In metaphysics we call this *chemicalization.* In psychology it is referred to as "cognitive dissonance." In the case of the Prodigal Son, earthly things had to be shaken up before spiritual realization could occur.

He could not appreciate the significance of the abundance, joy, peace, love and comfort of his Father's House if he had never left it and experienced its opposite. The realization of what he had given up, and where he now found himself, can be seen as a shift in consciousness. He had to be shaken out of his comfort zone before he could "come to himself" and grow spiritually.

This was also the case with the end of my marriage. It had to end in order for me to step fully into the purpose I came here to fulfill. I discovered that I had been more devoted to promoting and supporting my spouse's ministry, dreams and purpose than completing what had been assigned to me by the Holy Spirit. I had to leave that *home*—or be kicked out of it—in order to find my home in God and keep the promise I had made.

Similarly, there is the journey of my own "Prodigal Daughter" who left home (or was kicked out as she truly perceives it) at age 16 and began an unbelievable journey into a Street-Life adventure I had never imagined for her but was the evolution of a Soul Plan

---

[17] *The Hidden Parables: Activating the Secrets of the Gospels,* Todd Michael, 2008.

9

predesigned by her that led to a dramatic awakening, literally, that carried her toward fulfilling the purpose for which the journey was involved.

We are each called to bring forth the knowledge of the Light of Awareness into the physical world in order to facilitate transformation and fulfill our roles as co-creators.

> *So we, when our eyes begin to open to the light of Truth, are led back by Spirit, step by step, to our original oneness with God.*[18]

The first step the *Prodigal Son* took was to question his identity. He was unable to define himself in his father's house because he had never experienced anything other than his father's house and could only identify himself as a member of the household. To understand what *home* meant, he had to experience something other than where he was at that moment in time. He could not see his place in the family while he was *in* the family; he had to view it from another perspective—that of being outside of it altogether.

I'm sure you can think of a situation in your life where you were too close to it to be able to really see it; it wasn't until you stepped back to see it objectively that you could see the big picture.

Because we are still living in a world of duality, it is necessary to experience the opposite of living with God to fully appreciate what it means to actually live with God. Ultimately, as we move more towards the awakened consciousness, we will no longer need the lessons of duality.

Our journey here on this planet is not unlike that of the *Prodigal Son*. We are living simultaneously in two realms of existence—perfection and illusion or heaven and hell—the world of duality. The duality only appears in our misperception that we

---

[18] *Metaphysical Bible Dictionary*, Unity House, 1931, page 318.

are separate from God; that God is out there somewhere and we are in here all by ourselves. The illusion has become so real that we have convinced ourselves that there is not enough to go around and that if our Brother has much, we have less. We continually straddle the fence between the world of Truth and the word of physical experience or the physical senses. Dr. Fred Alan Wolf calls this "dancing on the edge of chaos."

He says "dancing on the edge of chaos" is exciting to us because of our tendency to be bored with what is safe or good for us. We are compelled to risk our health, our lives and even our financial stability for the thrill of the risk; the very threat of harm, injury or loss makes it exciting."[19]

What if we could do anything we wanted without any repercussions at all? Dr. Wolf says we would become bored and life would have absolutely no meaning or interest for us. It is the unknown that makes our lives worthwhile. It is also what causes us to cling to a world of duality—we just might experience the opposite and that makes life an adventure. To understand the spiritual significance of this we, like the Prodigal Son, must discover who we are and how we fit in this world—in the family of humanity.

To begin discovering our place in the cosmos we begin with the questions: "Who am I?" "Why am I here?" "Where do I fit in the scheme of things?"

To answer that let us go back to the "beginning" as expressed in the first chapter of John:

In the beginning was the Word and the Word was with God, and the Word was God.[20] ~ John 1:1

---

[19] http://www.soundstrue.com/store/dr-quantum-presents-107-132.html

[20] *Harper's Study Bible NSRV*, Zondervan. 1991.

Then the word was dispersed and made flesh and could relate within its Self. And in doing so, space and time were born. With space came distance. Separation was perceived. And with time, that separation was believed and God became estranged within ItsSelf. The first Word, the One Word, had appeared to become the many, and the outbreath was complete.

We are the Word made flesh; the outward expression of Divine Mind—the evolution of that which was first involved. We are the idea in the Mind of God. That which created us wanted to know Itself as an outward expression and we are here to express our Creator. In fact, we were made in Its image and likeness and endowed with all of Its attributes. We are co-creators in every sense of the *word*. Pun definitely intended.

It is said that we are below God and above the Angels and have been given dominion over all the things of the earth. Dominion is authority and authority makes us in charge of our lives in a very profound way. We *are* the Word; therefore, when we *speak* the Word—whether mentally or verbally—our authority establishes what we have spoken to be so.

Who am I? I am a living, breathing expression of Creative Principle (God). Why am I here? I am here to express the power and magnificence of Creative Principle (God) in all that I think, say and do in every aspect of my life. Where do I fit in the scheme of things? I am Creative Principle's (God's) perfect idea and greatest expression. I am responsible for all of Creative Principle's (God's) other creations. I am the Caretaker.

Wow! Doesn't that just take your breath away? To imagine that we are that powerful and that significant in the hierarchy of creation almost makes us shake in our boots. To realize that we have been given the responsibility of continuing the legacy of co-creation instills terror within us.

What makes it particularly challenging for us is that we are under the impression that we are pitifully weak individuals who are an island unto ourselves, alone and forced to fend for ourselves in this harsh, cruel world. We live in fear of each other as a result of the misperception that we are separate from God and one another. That is because the Divine Essence of our being is currently dysfunctional.

In Gnostic scriptures, there is a reference to the *Self-Willed One*, which I believe is the epitome of the definitive construct of our lives as pre-awakened humans. Our lives are motivated and driven by our desire for self-satisfaction through acquisition, accomplishment and competition. If so, who are we competing against if we are all one? Might this indicate that we are competing with ourselves? If all that we are competing with is our self, wouldn't that be an inordinate waste of time?

As self-willed, or ego-driven, we push against the obvious to have things be the way we want them to be regardless of blatant signposts indicating a better way. We are led into a repeating pattern of pain and suffering manifesting as challenges that continually bring us to our knees. We constantly find ourselves putting out fires, plugging up the holes in our lives and feeling the heavy frustration of it all. Ultimately, we must arrive at the conclusion that doing it "My Way" is not getting us anywhere. It was a big hit for Frank Sinatra but it may be time to stop making it our theme song. It may be time to surrender to the Will of our Creator—our Spiritual Intelligence—and let It point out the less treacherous way: the way to the Kingdom of God, which our Elder Brother indicated was within us, that provides us with the knowledge, wisdom and tools to build the Kingdom of Heaven right here right now, which is our Home.

The characteristics of the self-willed consciousness are quite evident in the story of the *Prodigal Son*. By his decision to leave home, he was clearly acting on his own selfish desires with no regard for how his decision might affect those around him.

In 1992 my daughter ran away from home because she didn't want to live by rules of any kind. She wanted to be free to do whatever she wanted to do and often brought serious repercussions to bear upon those of us around her. Once, she stole my car to go joy-riding and totaled it, leaving me without transportation to get to jobs or performances and causing a severe economic crisis in our lives. Acting upon her own selfish desires, she gave no thought to the consequences of her actions upon others around her.

As self-willed, we clumsily plow through life trampling everything in our path with no regard for the impact or impression we are making upon those around us and, on an even larger scale, the collective consciousness. My very dear friend, Dr. Gail Derin, once told me: "We are dangerous when we are oblivious to the effect we have upon others."

The opening phrase in the Book of John reminds us that there is an inextricable link between every living and non-living thing in existence. By existence, I mean that which we can see with the human eye as well as the minute particles of energy we cannot see. As we move further along as a species in the course of conscious evolution, we awaken to the reality of the interdependence of all energy and the fact that it is upon our awareness of this that the healing and survival of the planet rests.

So, how do we answer these questions and how do we discover our place in the cosmos? Simply put, we answer those questions by first understanding what we are "not" and then allowing ourselves to be fully present to what is *now* while embracing and accepting our humanness in the midst of it.

We begin to pay particular attention to the dynamics between what we are holding in consciousness and what we see playing out in our world and discover that there is a direct correlation between what is within and what is without. I teach my students that we are here to experience what we are *not* in order to discover *who we are.*

As we notice that we are not merely human beings, but spiritual beings having a spiritual experience on a human plane in a body, we come to the realization that our challenges and suffering play a major part in the unfolding of our spiritual journey.

We become aware that we are walking between two worlds and purposefully decide to completely experience both but from a different perspective.

By taking ourselves out of the experience and becoming the observer of what is the experience and what is not the experience, we demonstrate what Paul referred to as being "in the world but not of the world." We begin to live mindfully taking care to, first, do no harm.

Rev. Robert Brumet says "the more we awaken as individuals, the more we discover that we are <u>not</u> individuals at all."[21] Our journey home, then, begins with what *A Course in Miracles* speaks of as *remembering* in order to undo the *forgetting* that has fostered the illusion of separation from God. Now our task becomes that of reconnecting with *The Father*—our Creator.

Nature is a great teacher and starting point for learning this because we are drawn to the beauty and innocence of nature. By observing nature, we practice being The Observer. Here is a simple process that will bring this home and give you a basic experience of being The Observer.

---

[21] "Conscious Evolution Course", Rev. Robert Brumet, Unity Village, 1998.

EXERCISE:

Take any object of beauty (I prefer a rose) to a place where you will not be disturbed. Hold it in your hand or place it in something that allows you to observe it fully. Begin to simply gaze at it, just as you would gaze at anything; however, after a minute or so, begin to notice all of the intricate details of the object; i.e., its shape, size, color, texture, fragrance (if it has one) and so forth. Then begin to appreciate its make-up and composition. Finally, look at how you feel in your heart and in your body as you observe it. Now, simply appreciate it for what it is, without judgment. That is mindfulness. Do this once a day for 21 days and then begin looking at everything around you that way. That is being The Observer. This is also a form of Contemplation known in the practice of the Mystics.

A PRAYER

God of my being: support me in seeing my place in the world and in connecting with that point where we live as one. As I walk through the days of my life, clear my vision of those things that separate us and direct my sight toward only that which reminds me of my true relationship to every living thing upon this planet. I am so grateful.

Amen

AN AFFIRMATION

(Repeat this affirmation 7 times a day for 7 days)

I am the beloved child of a rich, loving and forgiving Parent
whose good pleasure is to give me the Kingdom of Heaven.
In gratitude I accept my Divine Inheritance NOW.

STUDY QUESTIONS:

1. How has evolution in consciousness changed life on the planet?
2. Can you identify any noticeable evolution in consciousness over the last 20 years? If yes, describe it.
3. How have you personally evolved in consciousness?
4. What things have you done in your life to experience yourself apart from family, friends, society, culture, etc? What was the result? What did you discover? What did you learn?
5. As you look back on your life, have there been any clues that your experiences (good or bad) were purposeful and had some meaning with regard to where you are today?

II

THE ILLUSION OF DUALITY

STEP TWO — Belief in one's ability to escape from the Father—Pain is Inevitable; Suffering is Optional

[13]*"And not many days after, the younger son gathered all together, and took his journey into a far country and there soon wasted his inheritance on riotous living".* (Luke 15:13)

And the journey begins. . .

The *Prodigal Son* (the Soul) has taken his inheritance and gone off to a "far country." Metaphysically, the *Far Country* represents anything that separates us in consciousness from the Source—The Father's House or The Father. It is our *belief* or perception that we are on our own, alone, and have nothing to depend upon except ourselves. When we reach this state of consciousness we begin to look to outer things to fulfill our needs and erroneously perceive a limited availability of resources. What we believe, then, becomes our reality—our experience.

In his desire to leave his Father's house the *Prodigal Son* began to experience the opposite of the life he had known and to which he had become accustomed. Because he had only known one lifestyle, anything other than that became the *opposite* experience. He was naturally thrown into comparisons of "what is" with "what was." We can only surmise, based on subsequent verses that his experiences took on a dualistic paradigm of good/bad, easy/hard, right/wrong and joy/pain. No longer under the protective covering of a loving family and being shielded from the difficulties of life, he could now truly know the difference between "home" and "not-home."

One of my favorite books is *Little Soul and the Sun*[22] by Neale Donald Walsch. In it a Little Soul is having an identity crisis of sorts and, in a conversation with God, tells God that he knows who he is—The Light—but also that he wants to *experience* himself as "the Light." Much to his dismay, God advises him that, in order to experience himself as "the Light," it is necessary to also experience "darkness" so he can actually *know* the difference. Ultimately, he decided that the Light he wanted to experience himself as being was the "Light of Forgiveness." For this, it required leaving Heaven/God and journeying through the World of Humanity where he would meet another Soul who agreed to give him something to forgive so that he could experience himself as the "Light of Forgiveness."

Such is our journey as Souls. We are seeking to know ourselves; however, knowing that we are Spiritual Beings, made in the image and likeness of that which created us, is not enough at our current level of conscious evolution. Due to our naturally inquisitive cellular nature, we seek to join, to connect with others and experience ourselves in relation to that which we believe is "not us." We learn who we are or who we are not by what we perceive in the world and in other people.

---

[22] *The Little Soul and The Sun*, Neale Donald Walsch, Hampton Roads Publishing, 1998.

Ken Wilbur calls this "drawing boundary lines" and says that:

> *"…by doing so we progressively limit our world and turn from our true nature in order to embrace boundaries. Our originally pure and unitive consciousness then functions on varied levels, with different identities and different boundaries. These different levels are basically the many ways we can and do answer the questions, "Who am I?"*[23]

This is the experience of incarnating into a world of duality where we come to experience what we are *not* in order to discover, understand and experience who we *are*.

What is duality? How did it begin?

The dictionary refers to *Duality* as a "dichotomy"—a system of twos, pairs, opposites such as right and left, up and down, dark and light, good and bad/evil, etc. When there is one thing, there has to be a thing that is its opposite or other half.

Duality shows up in every aspect of our lives. Whether we are referring to scientific laws (action vs reaction), Universal Laws (logical vs illogical), mental perceptions and beliefs (right vs wrong) or physical sense experience (good vs bad), duality is always present.

From a scientific perspective, *Duality* exists as part of the natural consequence of living in a universe structured on a design of polar opposites that sustain a balanced system: up/down; right/left; dark/light; hot/cold; in/out. These scientific constructs have caused us to further elaborate upon those opposites within the arena of our perceptions: good/evil; right/wrong; beauty/ugliness; full/empty; and a long list of other perceptions. In the arena of our physical experiences, we have accepted that there is an opposite for everything we experience. We have even gone so far as to base

---

[23] *No Boundary: Eastern and Western Approaches to Personal Growth*, Ken Wilbur, Shambala, 2001.

our religious doctrines upon these opposites as a determinant of whether someone fits within the acceptable parameters of those doctrines and, of course, we attribute them to God.

Genesis 1:5 tells us that God divided the void into light (day) and dark (night), placing the sun by day and the moon by night. From that we have built a planetary existence based on these opposites. In fact, our lives appear to be governed by them.

This system of opposites can either lock us into continuous struggle to overcome the challenges the opposites present or support us in realizing the Truth of our being. They can limit us to perpetual judgment or elevate us to a higher level of appreciation.

> *If we never experience the chill of a dark winter, it is very unlikely that we will ever cherish the warmth of a bright summer's day. Nothing stimulates our appetite for the simple joys of life more than the starvation caused by sadness or desperation. In order to complete our amazing life journey successfully, it is vital that we turn each and every dark tear into a pearl of wisdom, and find the blessing in every curse.* [24]

Charles Fillmore believed that it was our material thoughts that actually perpetuated the concept of *duality*. He states:

> *The material universe is a malformation, a limited idea of spiritual substance, along with its duality and polarity; e.g. good and evil. We continue to perpetuate the material universe by our material thoughts.* [25]

---

[24] *Divine Living: The Essential Guide To Your True Destiny*, Indigo House, Anthon St. Maarten, 2012.

[25] *Fillmore Truth Kernel 04*, Orren Evans Ministries, Inc. Reverend Orren Evans, Minister, Irving, TX, June 1995.

As if to verify this, recently my Senior Minister, Rev. David McArthur, offered a concrete demonstration in service one Sunday when speaking on "Full and Over-flowing." He held up a glass of water and asked what we saw. Most responses were: "Half-Full." One would naturally expect this in a Unity or New Thought church. As his message continued to unfold, he led us to the awareness of the unlimited energy existent within universal law and Truth: There is always more than enough and the glass is always "full and overflowing."

What he was pointing out was how our perception governs the outcome or manifestation of energy into the material world. If we believe the glass is "half empty" that will be our relationship to law and the outcome of our experience. Conversely, if we believe the glass is "full and overflowing" our experience will reflect the same.

In other words while there *is* a design of polar opposites, because we have been endowed with the power to create and have dominion over the things of the earth," (Gen 1: 1-26), we can move beyond the confines of *duality* and achieve or manifest without boundaries.

In Radical Forgiveness, we practice the process of being *willing* to see the perfection in every situation, regardless of how it is currently playing out. This means it is neither good nor bad—it just is—and we create a space for it to be what it is without criticism, condemnation or judgment. When we withhold the energy of making it anything in particular, we allow it to continue its movement through our lives to fulfill the purpose for which it showed up. By giving it no energy, we allow it to unfold in Divine Order.

A great story, once told by my former husband as a Teach-Point in one of his Sunday Lessons, beautifully illustrates this:

> *There was a Taoist farmer, whose horse somehow broke through the corral and ran away. The farmer's friends*

and neighbors exclaimed: "Oh! That was the only horse you had to help you with the plowing and other chores. That is awful." The farmer replied: "Maybe so, maybe not." A few days later, the horse came back, bringing with it two more wild horses. The farmer's friends and neighbors exclaimed: "What a blessing. That is just wonderful." The farmer replied: Maybe so, maybe not." Not too long after, the farmer's son was kicked by one of the wild horses and broke his leg. The friends and neighbors exclaimed: "That's just awful. Such bad luck." The farmer replied: "Maybe so, maybe not." Very soon, the army showed up to recruit his son to go to war but passed over him because of the broken leg. The friends and neighbors exclaimed: "What good fortune." The farmer replied: "Maybe so, maybe not."

There is always something playing out that we cannot see from our limited perspective. If we withhold our judgments and emotional attachments as it unfolds, it will follow the path of the Divine Plan and manifest in the right and perfect manner for our highest good and the spiritual growth and evolution in consciousness conscripted by the Soul. In the case of the *Prodigal Son,* there was a spiritual big picture playing out that he would understand later.

Most of us have grown up with the belief in *Good* and *Evil.* We were taught that people are either good or evil; that there is a pervasive evil upon this earth; that we are sinners at our core and must be redeemed by the acceptance of Jesus Christ as our Lord and Savior or we go to hell when we die. Our work, then, becomes striving to *not* be evil while recognizing the evil in others and in the world.

While we cannot deny that the *energy of evil* exists, we must look at it in the greater context of the cosmological concept of duality and the design of polar opposites that creates the balance of all existence. The *opposites* simply exist. The experience of them is facilitated by our thoughts, beliefs, emotions and choices. We can live in a realm where the darker, heavier energy exists but we are not required to have them as part of our experience. Seeing the evidence of the existence of something and actually experiencing it are based on *choice.*

What do I mean by this?

As we operate within this system of duality, we have a choice moment by moment to take an action or speak words that either align with dark energy or light energy—good or evil—and our experience will reflect what we have chosen and, subsequently, what we draw to us in the future will reflect that choice.

I was on a bus in Sacramento and overheard a conversation between three men, who were bragging about how they would walk behind a guy in their neighborhood, who was always dropping money out of his pocket or wallet, and taking great delight in the fact that they never told him about it or returned his money to him. I am fairly certain they had absolutely no idea they had aligned with *dark energy*, setting them up to experience same in their lives. Possibly, in the days and months to come, they would have a difficult time understanding the things that were happening to them. In fact, it might even manifest as a difficulty with holding onto money.

The System of Opposites keeps the energy fairly balanced. It is governed by Universal Laws, is neutral and operates without regard to one's status and without judgment. There is *evil* in the world. It is not, however, our nature. At birth we are whole and perfect, untainted by things outside of us. We revel in getting all of our needs met and our wants satisfied. We cry and someone comes to fulfill our every desire: feed us, change our diapers or simply hold us so we feel loved. We are the rulers of our empire, our *babydom.* Then something happens. . .

Our caregivers, culture, society, community and family begin to teach us to identify our lives and ourselves based upon a system of opposites: good and evil/bad, right and wrong, acceptable and unacceptable and the like. Everything is experienced based on these opposites—this system of duality.

We begin to compartmentalize our characteristics and attributes based on what is acceptable and what is unacceptable as determined by what makes people either love us or reject us. Colin Tipping refers to these compartments or divisions as *Cool* and *Uncool*. That which is acceptable and gets us love forms the mask or persona we present to the world, and gets stored in the *Cool* compartment. That which is unacceptable and causes us to be rejected is hidden away and gets stored in the *Uncool* compartment and becomes our *Shadow Stuff*.

By *Shadow Stuff*, I mean the collection of identities, personas and subpersonalities that are formed as a result of what is hidden by the Mask we wear in order to be acceptable or "Cool." Our *Shadow* is made up of the rejected aspects of us that don't go away and have a tendency to surface when our defenses are down and we are riding high on a wave of false security built upon an artificial persona orchestrated by an army of *Core Negative Beliefs*. Robert Bly refers to our shadow as the "long bag we drag behind us[26]."

Debbie Ford says this about our shadow:

"When you embrace your shadow you will no longer have to live in fear. Find the gifts of your shadow and you will finally revel in all the glory of your true self. Then you will have the freedom to create the life you have always desired."[27]

---

[26] *A Little Book on the Human Shadow*, Robert Bly, Harper, San Francisco, 1988.
[27] *Dark Side of the Light Chasers*, Debbie Ford, Putnam, 1998.

We have witnessed the outward manifestation of *Shadow Stuff* through the upheavals in the lives of Tiger Woods, Governor Mark Sanford, Senator John Edwards, Lindsey Lohan and others as we watch their carefully-constructed personas disintegrate before our very eyes. What we are witnessing is those aspects of themselves they locked away (or thought they had) rising to the surface to take their rightful place in the forefront of their lives.

Yes, I said *rightful place.* Identifying and integrating our *Shadow Stuff* is what makes us whole. Until that is accomplished, they are our *Unlived Life* as Robert Johnson calls it. He goes on to say:

> *"The shadow is that which has not entered adequately into consciousness. It is the despised quarter of our being. It often has an energy potential nearly as great as that of our ego."*[28]

For example, a child who is constantly chided for not being more like a sibling who others label as "the good one" or "sweet and unselfish" and in turn labels this child as "bad" or "mean and selfish" that child will make a determination. This determination or decision is that being *good, nice* and *unselfish* is a way of getting love and they will put all of their energies into creating a persona that aligns with what others want them to be and gets them the love they seek.

They will end up as either *servaholics,* overachievers or become chronic doormats for anyone they feel will provide them with that love they desire. The "catch," however, is that while they are working overtime to prove they are what others want them to be they are at the same time resenting the hell out of having to be that

---

[28] *Owning Your Own Shadow,* Robert A. Johnson, Harper Collins, 1993.

way. They hate themselves for the hypocrisy and are angry with those they perceive are forcing them to be that way.

The really sad thing about it is that, when they either rebel or attempt to change, everyone hates them for not continuing the hoax they have previously perpetrated. In other words, they are damned if they do and damned if they don't. Such is the dilemma perpetuated by the World of Duality.

How do we discover this *Shadow Stuff?* Tolle says we should ask the questions: *What is false in me?*

We must have the courage to open the door to the forbidden rooms within our unconscious level of mind to see what has been repressed or suppressed and be willing to embrace them as part of our wholeness. To be whole means accepting and loving even the *Uncool* parts of us. They may bring a balance to our lives that were previously missing.

For example, if we have spent our lives giving ourselves away — then being a little selfish, honoring our own needs, taking time for ourselves, paying attention to what our heart is calling for—is essential to regaining our wholeness and joy and establishing our own self-worth.

As we live, learn and grow through this world of duality, it is extremely important that we not lose sight of the fact that something bigger is playing out than we can see from our limited human perspective. There is a spiritual big picture playing out that is available for viewing by anyone who is willing to pay the price of admission: a shift in perception. By seeing the opposite as perfect just the way it is, we cause a shift in how we perceive the world—and ourselves—and the quantum mechanics of the universe arranges the subatomic particles to match our new perception that: there is nothing *wrong* happening out there, only something *wrong* happening within our perception about what is happening out there.

Eckhart Tolle, in writing about his Dark Night of the Soul in *The Power of Now*, says "I understood that the intense pressure of suffering that night must have forced my consciousness to withdraw from its identification with the unhappy and deeply fearful self. . .this withdrawal must have been so complete that this false, suffering self immediately collapsed…"[29] Those great challenges that bring the *experience* of pain and suffering are often the catalyst for our awakening. We are so beaten down, having tried everything we humanly knew to help ourselves without success that we are more open, reachable, teachable and healable than when we are riding high on the stage of the theater built by our persona. That is when we can hear the beeping of the homing signal and the Voice of God saying "Come Home."

I had been so angry and hurt following the abrupt end of my marriage that, for months, I had found myself verbally cursing out (on an almost daily basis) the man I blamed for my pain and suffering. I curled up in a ball at night sobbing so deeply it felt like my insides were going to spill out onto the bed or carpet. One night, I was in so much pain that I found myself on the floor with my forehead on the carpet just knowing that I was going to die right then and there. It was so painful that it felt as if the very skin on my body was being ripped away strip by strip. It was as if everything I had identified with—had thought I was—was being stripped away, as if my entire body and self were being burned alive, when suddenly I saw my Soul and I knew. I knew that everything that had happened to me—not just the end of the marriage—was preparing me for what was beyond that moment. I could see that my entire journey with my husband was not about the suffering, but about what was to come. It was a Rite of Passage toward fulfilling the purpose for which I had chosen to incarnate in this lifetime. It was, therefore, purposeful and had

---

[29] *Power of Now*, Eckhart Tolle, Namaste Publishing, 1999, page 5.

great meaning and it was no longer necessary to suffer. So, I got up and began moving toward Now.

It is absolutely true that we have experiences of pain and suffering upon this playing field of polarity; however, we can choose to see the perfection—or at least be willing to do so—and witness the cosmic shift in our lives or continue to play out a life of suffering. Either choice is still absolutely perfect and will lead, ultimately, to the same conclusion. It all comes down to our right to *choose* and the experience we wish to have.

> *The deep suffering appears to lead us to another level of awareness—why?—it takes us out of the world into the depths of the suffering—it forces us to look for something beyond ourselves because our "self" has led us to the suffering.*[30]

In our struggle to hold on to those "perks" of being human, we lose contact with the Real part of us that provides us with the perks that bring heaven into this human realm without the consequences of pain and suffering. It is unknown to us at a conscious level and we fear that which is unknown. We don't realize that it is possible to co-exist peacefully and joyfully in both realms simultaneously.

How do we live successfully in a world of opposites without succumbing to pain and suffering?

By "walking between the worlds"[31] as Gregg Braden's book of that same name so powerfully teaches; by living as if everything that occurs is happening *for* us rather than *to* us. If all experience is a gift, or opportunity for learning, healing and expanding

---

[30] *The Power of Now*, Eckhart Tolle, Namaste Publishing, 1999.
[31] *Walking Between Worlds: The Science of Compassion*, Gregg Braden, Radio Bookstore Press, 1997.

consciousness, we either avoid victimhood altogether or only briefly visit that experience before stepping fully into our power.

In *Radical Forgiveness*[32], there is a Four-Step Process we may use in the midst of a challenge or upsetting situation when there is no time to complete a Worksheet. It could even be referred to as a "Portable Worksheet." The process is quick, easy and extremely effective:

1. Wow! Look what I created.
2. I notice my feelings and judgments and love myself for having them.
3. I am willing to see the perfection in this situation.
4. I choose the power of peace.

If I created this then I cannot be a victim and a creator at the same time. The moment I recognize my power to create and re-create my life I am no longer a victim. Noticing and accepting my feelings and acknowledging that I am making judgments about the situation, even if I don't know what they are, prevents the self-defeating act of condemning myself for having these feelings and judgments, taking me another step away from victimhood and toward my power. Stating to the Universe my *willingness* to see the situation as perfect, even if I can't at that moment, opens the way for the perfection to reveal itself when the time is right. Finally, choosing peace instead of any of its opposites stills the chaos that might be swirling around me or within me.

My daughter was extremely happy to see how well this 4-Step Process worked when she was attempting to get her estranged husband to help pay for their son's after-school program. She had been embroiled in conflict with him about it and, realizing she was getting nowhere, gave up saying: "Never mind, I'll take care

---

[32] *Radical Forgiveness*, Colin Tipping, 13 Global Publications, 1997.

of it." She hung up the phone and did the 4-Step Process once and then repeated it a second time. Within 3 minutes he called back and said he would pay for it.

Colin Tipping says we must have "double vision." We must witness what is occurring in the present moment but also be aware of the Spiritual Big Picture being played out *for* us (even if we can't see it at the time) despite the appearance.

The Spiritual Big Picture playing out for my daughter was the opportunity to discover that *force* gets us nowhere, as it is a relinquishing of our power; however, choosing peace is taking back our power. She had to give up the resistance in order to win.

The end of my marriage appeared to me and many others as a really terrible thing. What we could not see in the Spiritual Big Picture was that, although together he and I could do some awesome work to further the cause of Truth, separately, we could cover more territory. We had completed that part of the journey from the point at which our paths merged and now we were taking divergent paths leading to the next stage in our spiritual walk. We had fulfilled our Soul Contract.

Everyone is influenced by the dual nature of the stage set we designed to play out this human role and the drama unfolding upon it can be fun, painful, enlightening and entertaining at the same time. The key to having the experience our Soul requires for its growth, without the suffering we find ourselves in after pitching a tent in the pain, is to consciously choose to see both simultaneously—the world of human interaction and the world of Truth and Divine Connection. They are not the same thing.

The world of human interaction, or *real* world as we will refer to it, is that which we see and experience with our five senses; we can taste it, touch it, smell it, see it and hear it. The World of Truth and Divine Connection, or *World of Reality* as we will call it here, is that world of Absolute Truth. It never changes; it is the same today as yesterday and will be the same tomorrow; and it never disappoints us or causes us to suffer. One brings suffering and the other brings joy. In his book, Colin Tipping refers to these two worlds as "The World of Humanity" and "The World of Divine Truth."

Gregg Braden refers to them as External Technology: The First Path, and Internal Technology: The Second Path.[33]

It is impossible not to experience pain when living as humans; however, although pain is inevitable suffering is optional. Our choice to live in one world or the other determines our experience.

> *Pain is when the hurt (physical, mental or emotional) occurs. Suffering is when we take up residence in the pain.*[34]

Whether to have a perfectly normal experience of pain, that comes for a time and then moves us toward our healing, or to submerge ourselves in suffering is based on *choice.* The "choice" is based on our willingness to shift our vision beyond what is *real,* to perceive what Reality is.

We can use that one statement from the *Radical Forgiveness 4-Step Process* as almost a mantra: *I am willing to see the perfection in this.* I am willing. I may not be able to see it but I am willing. Nothing more. Nothing less. Simply willing.

A Course in Miracles invites us to offer our "little willingness" to the Holy Spirit/The Universe and it will bring together all of its powers to support us in having it be so. All we need is to be willing to be willing and in the space of that *willingness* there is an opening for a shift in our perception that just might help us

---

[33] *Walking Between Worlds*, Gregg Braden, Radio Bookstore Press, 1997.

[34] *Messages: Essays on a Spiritual Journey*, Sheila Gautreaux-Lee, Author House, 2005, p 158.

move beyond the pain of the present to the gift wrapped within it; thus, causing a shift in consciousness.

Consciously living life in that way teaches us to utilize duality to our benefit rather than be at the effect of a cause we cannot fathom. That makes us "masters of our fate" and "captains of our soul." [35] It took me many years to grow into the understanding of this poem by William Ernest Hensley. I memorized it in high school and had no understanding of how it would impact me in the future. And as I grew in consciousness, I grew into this poem. Through the many nights that covered me, I discovered my unconquerable soul. It was the journey that encompassed much duality that led me to understand how to "captain my soul".

The *Prodigal Son* has taken his inheritance and gone to the *far country* where he has wasted it. We can surmise that he has partied and picked up the tab for his temporary friends and now has nothing left. In his ignorance of what it took for his Father to acquire and maintain his wealth and the love with which it was given, he is now bankrupt. Yet we cannot judge him too harshly, as he has just begun the journey of awakening to the Truth of his own being.

Since this is our story, and the *Prodigal Son* represents us in our immature and un-awakened consciousness, there is a powerful Teach-Point here.

Our *inheritance* is something with which we have been blessed by God and the blessing God gives us is that of *divine ideas,* which Charles Fillmore says manifest in the outer expression as our *good.* "It is the underlying idea back of any expression."[36]

Wasting our inheritance means bypassing the blessing from God to follow the dictates of our ego-driven wants. The divine ideas of God are ever-flowing, ever-present, in the universe and

---

[35] "Invictus", William Ernest Henley. [See Appendix II for the full poem].

[36] *Dynamics for Living*, Charles Fillmore, Unity School of Christianity, 1967, page 48.

in our lives and are available to us for use in producing our good. When we don't make use of them we are *wasting* them. When we use them frivolously or to cause harm, we are *wasting* them.

Each time we focus our attention on what is not the Source (job, paycheck, stock market, help from others, etc.) we are focusing on the ways through which our Source expresses instead of the means, which *is* our Source. We are, therefore, *wasting our inheritance.*

The *Prodigal Son* had available to him a never-ending, inexhaustible resource of powerful ways in which to utilize his status in the Son-ship to create abundance and have a life of joy, peace and perfection; however, he chose to live according to the *real world* instead of the *World of Reality.*

Do we not frequently succumb to the same thing? Each of us is given an abundance of gifts, talents and skills for use to manifest prosperity into our lives and likewise contribute to the collective; however, when things get difficult, we forget about our Source and get trapped by an erroneous perception that our *good* comes from a job, a paycheck or other people. When these things are not available to us, we find ourselves in pain and, ultimately, suffering.

Right now we are witnessing the rampant fear, doubt, anger and hopelessness permeating the collective consciousness upon our planet as more and more people have lost their jobs and their homes. Those who have jobs and homes are living in constant fear that at any moment they, too, could be in the same boat. They live constantly afraid of losing that job or paycheck. Like the *Prodigal Son*, they forget that God is the only job or paycheck that will sustain them even in times of the worst economic state.

As a side note, I must give the *Prodigal Son* credit for having the courage and faith to *ask* for his inheritance from his father. He felt he had a right to it and demanded that it be given to him. We allow our subconscious beliefs of unworthiness to prevent us from even asking our Father (God). What caused the suffering of the *Prodigal Son* was the unawareness of the blessed nature of the inheritance, his misperception of separation and his Core Negative Beliefs that caused him to *waste* it.

> *An example we see often in lottery winners is how soon all the money they have won is lost. Their "new found benefits" are lost to extravagant spending, "riotous living", family and friends showing up (much like the Prodigal Son's friends) with their hands out, and not being mindful of their new-found wealth. The reason this is so common, is that the Core Negative Beliefs are still there; they do not change just because outer circumstances have changed. If the Core Negative Beliefs are residing in lack and limitation, no matter the circumstances, the "benefits" will not hang around for very long.*

What then is *riotous living?* It definitely indicates being out of control or without guidance or direction. When we forget to connect with the Source of all our good, our lives get out of control, we are without guidance and we lose our direction. The *Prodigal Son* pursues the path of his ego, which causes him to overlook the divine ideas flowing in and through him, and he finds his life has taken a direction over which he has no control. In other words, somewhere he took a wrong turn and got off course.

> *Vivian wanted to save her marriage and came to me with that objective in mind. She had cheated on her husband and they were trying to find their way back. As with all my clients, I made it clear to her that my role was not to insure that they stayed together; my objective was to see that they were each healed so they*

could make the decision to stay or not from a healed place. During the course of the coaching process her husband Sam was healed but Vivian was so fixated on saving the marriage she missed the opportunity to heal her own life and the marriage ended. If she had put the time and effort in healing her past wounds that instigated the infidelity in the first place, Sam may have felt a real shift was possible for them and been willing to work toward keeping the marriage together. It was a clear indication to Sam that the infidelity would occur again because the root cause had not been healed.

The concept of living consciously aware of being in two worlds simultaneously reminds me of the old saying about not being able to see the forest for the trees. Because the *Real World* is so pronounced, obvious and constantly in our faces, it is difficult to take our eyes and mind off the entertainment so we can get to the blessing. In other words, we must chop down the trees that have overrun our minds so we can view the beautiful forest.

The world of duality serves a scientific function as a principle of balance in the universe. The world of Truth serves a spiritual function as a corrective principle in consciousness when our lives are off course and we find ourselves *dancing on the edge of chaos.*

The key to successfully living in this world of polar opposites is remembering that God exists within the light and the dark; that there is only God, only Truth, and all else is but a hoax perpetrated by our ego for its own glorification. In our spiritual work, we say the EGO is "Edging God Out". Each time we look to the ego for our guidance and support we move further away from our conscious connection to God. Like the *Prodigal Son*, we waste our precious inheritance on riotous living.

God, Spirit, is the only presence in the universe, and is the only power. It is in, through and around all creation as its life and sustaining power. We must seek only after God—keep our eyes on the prize—and stay on course.

Our lives lose direction the moment they cease to be a voyage for the discovery of God.[37]

The second step toward home is learning to walk between the *Real World* and the *World of Reality* or, as Biblical Scripture implies in Romans 12:2 and John 15:19, that, while we are definitely *in* the world, we are not *of* this world. This means having an awareness of that which is *within* us regardless of what is *before* us. We must be attuned to the Truth of God—love, peace, health, joy, forgiveness, prosperity—as we witness and experience the outer conditions of our lives as they take place in the world we see. In other words, we must live *in* the world we see but live *by* the world we cannot see except in the inner places of our being. This begins with the realization that we are eternally linked with Divine Presence.

Jesus said: "The Father and I are One" ~ John 10:30

EXERCISE

Pull out a sheet of paper and write out three (3) questions, leaving space enough after each to insert answers. You may even choose to put each question at the top of a separate sheet of paper. The questions are:

What makes me an individual?
What makes me separate?
What's the difference?

---

[37] Author Unknown

Now find a quiet place where you won't be interrupted. Turn off the ringers on your cell phone or other nearby phones. Place the sheet with your questions next to you along with a pen or pencil so they are easy to use.

Close your eyes. Take a few deep cleansing breaths, remembering to breathe all the way down to the lower region of the stomach, and then breathe normally until you feel really relaxed. Don't struggle against thoughts as they come and go in your mind, just notice them and let them move on. When you feel really relaxed, ask the first question in your mind: What makes me an individual?"

Let the question sit there until words or images begin to form in your mind and then open your eyes and begin to write. There is no limit to the answer. Just write until you feel you've written all that comes to mind. Repeat the process for the next two (2) questions. When you have answered all the questions simply sit in the experience of the moment briefly. Take a deep cleansing breath and let a big sigh escape from your mouth. Open your eyes when you feel ready.

Review your answers at that time or later. When you do, notice what value, emphasis or identity you place upon things (or even people if they show up in your answers) and see whether you have allowed anything to stand between you and God or you and all creation. Use the following questions as a guide:

1. Do I identify myself by race, gender, age, religious beliefs, socio-economic status or some other socially-motivated classification? Does this identification separate me from others?

2. Did anything come up that provided you with insights as to how you separate yourself from family, friends, associates or community? If so, are they things you were taught early in life or that you learned as a result of life experiences?

3. Is there a difference between being an individual and being separate? Explain your answer.

When we are able to discover for ourselves the answers to these questions and personally experience our individuality while eliminating what keeps us in the mindset of *separation* we will have come closer to "home" than the *Prodigal Son* has at this stage of his journey. It is not our *Individuality* that makes us forget our place in the Cosmos and our relationship to everyone and everything, it is our belief in *separation*.

> *What we all need is a better understanding of the principles at the very foundation of Being, of the spiritual character of God, and especially of the omnipresence of the spiritual principles. Then we need to understand our relation to these spiritual principles and what we have to do to make them operative in our mind and affairs[38].*

Let us keep this in mind as we continue to follow the journey of the *Prodigal Son*. It will help clarify why this is definitely our journey as well.

A PRAYER

Dear God, it is my desire to live as one with you and all creation. If I have separated myself in any way, I forgive myself. Teach me how to live as one with you and every living thing on this planet and in the Universe. I am willing to embrace and accept that I am one with everything. Thank you for a closer walk with you along my journey home.

Amen

---

[38] *Teach us to Pray*, Charles Fillmore, Unity School of Christianity, 1945, p159.

AN AFFIRMATION

I am one with God and, therefore, one with all life

STUDY QUESTIONS

1. What was your original understanding of "good" and "evil" as it relates to God? Has that changed? If so, how?
2. What have you noticed, or are noticing, about the concept of duality in your life and in the world today?
3. Have you ever had an experience of your Oneness with God? How?
4. What beliefs about yourself can you clearly identify as resulting from conditioning (familial, cultural, religious, etc.)? How has it impacted your life?
5. Can you relate in any way to this phase of the *Prodigal Son's* journey? If so, how?

III

UNDERSTANDING
THE ONE WILL

STEP THREE — Surrender Your Will—Release the ego's grasp upon your mind.

¹⁴"And when he had spent all, there arose a mighty famine in that land; and he began to be in want. ¹⁵So he hired himself out to a local landowner where he found himself feeding the pigs. ~ Luke 15:14-15

The *Prodigal Son* is now in serious trouble. Not only has he spent all of his inheritance but now there is a famine in the land where he has gone to find himself—the Far Country. He finds himself "wanting" instead. What is it that he wants? Is it food, shelter, those friends who have by now deserted him because he has no more money to spend on them? Or is he "wanting" (longing) for home—the Father's house? The Father?

Could it be that when everything is stripped away, and there is nothing more to long for, that signal implanted within us before the world was, begins beeping as a call to come home? Might we be ready for the *Long Journey Home*?

That was exactly the case with my Dark Night of the Soul that occurred when the marriage ended. The experience was that of both a mental and physical stripping away, until I was left with nothing but God, and trust me, It had my attention. No one was there to intervene and there was no place to turn but to God and begin making that *Long Journey Home.*

How long is the journey home? It is as long as the distance between the head and the heart and depends upon how long it takes us to close the distance. The homing signal is calling for us to leave the restrictions of the head—the intellect—and return to the heart. Where we have previously depended upon the ego to direct our journey, we must now learn to open ourselves up to the intelligence of the heart where all true knowledge lies. No longer can we lean upon our own understanding; now we must surrender to the wisdom and guidance of the Holy Spirit.

Scripture says:

> *"Trust God with all your heart and lean not unto your own understanding."* ~ Proverbs 3:5

Our Journey, then, becomes about aligning not with our will but with God's Will. We must give up all personal will and give ourselves over to the Will and the Way of God. This is the One Will—the only Will. That is the strategy, the map, for getting us home.

But what is this thing called *Will*? How does it operate? We hear in all theologies about the *Will of God*. We also hear about developing and focusing our *willpower*. With whose *Will* are we aligning in making this journey? God's Will? Our Will?

In *The Revealing Word* Charles Fillmore says *"Will is the executive faculty in mind, the determining factor in [humanity]".*[39]

In other words, it is the policymaking, managerial, ability within one's mind that supports us in making decisions or *choosing* one direction over another. While this is the aspect of humankind that gives us *dominion* over our lives, it also puts us in a "Catch-22" situation.

The human experience is a dance between the Will of God and Free Will. Because we are first spiritual beings, we are preprogrammed with the attributes and characteristics of that which created us; however, as we live on a human plane, we also have the Free Will program running simultaneously. This sets up a very interesting state of affairs that requires us to make *choices* moment by moment and is not only challenging but can be tricky. Understanding what constitutes God's Will adds to the dilemma and then exercising our freedom of choice causes its own level of insanity – "dancing on the edge of chaos."

This very precarious dance often finds us making what we consider the easier of the two choices—doing what we want to do—and ending up like the *Prodigal Son* in a *far country* seemingly bereft of our support system and starving for what we *believe* we don't have. We find ourselves in a *famine.*

Famine, metaphysically, represents our lack of faith in God's ability to provide us with what we need, require or desire. It means we have strayed away from and lost sight of our true source and are seeking to be filled with things of a material nature.

I remember what it was like to lose everything I owned. When I was moving from Washington, DC, a friend had insisted that

---

[39] *The Revealing Word*, Charles Fillmore, Unity School of Christianity, 1959, page 209, [author's license].

I store my household furnishings in the three-car garage of the mansion-type home she rented while I looked for a place in New York City. I accepted in order to save myself the expense of storage fees. Some months later when I was ready to move my things to New York I discovered she had been evicted and somehow all of my things had disappeared. This included all of my children's baby pictures, mementos, family photographs, collectibles and valuable antiques. It knocked me for a loop until I realized, and rather quickly I might add, that God had made it possible for me to acquire all of those things so I was sure God would give them back to me and then some. I probably should have left off "and then some."

You see, we are never outside of God's generosity and willingness to give; therefore, we can never lose everything. Everything God has is ours as offspring and beneficiaries of God. As long as we recognize the One True Source of everything, the entire Universe is available to us.

In the last chapter we talked about the "self-willed one" and discussed the dynamics of living in a world of duality while discovering that we are one with our Creator and with all life both animate and inanimate. We learned that duality was a natural component of both the physical and non-physical world but that dividing ourselves occurs as we attempt to determine our place in the cosmos—the world—to fit in.

Much of what we experience in our struggle to live and work within the universal pattern of duality is a dance between joy and pain, thriving and suffering, and in the midst of the dance we discover and learn many things about both ourselves and the two worlds—physical and spiritual.

In *A Course in Miracles* it says:

> *"⁴Free will does not mean that you can establish the curriculum. ⁵It means only that you can elect what you want to take at a given time."*⁴⁰

What *The Course* more than hints at is that this world of duality is the classroom for our spiritual growth, for discovery and learning, for testing both the laws of humanity and principles of Truth in the laboratory of our lives. The experiences we encounter along the way make up the curriculum that provides us with many lessons to be learned. The people who show up as our adversaries, offering many opportunities to learn to forgive and love them, are our Master Teachers. In awakening to what they are actually there for, and love and discovering the gifts they are there to provide, we "remove the blocks to the awareness," of love's presence, and we earn our credits toward a degree in Oneness. That is the Will of God, which is actually "our Will" as *The Course* teaches us.

The Course says "there is only One Will." If this is so, we merely believe our will is separate from God's Will when we do something that is out of alignment. We are simply taking the scenic route in getting to the One Will. The road may be bumpy with lots of potholes but we *will* get there because "God's Will *is* my Will." The important thing to remember along the way is that God *wills* us home.

What is the One Will? How do we surrender to it?

The One Will may be looked at as a metaphor for tapping into what many teachers refer to as the Mind of God, which could be seen as a metaphor for the essence and substance of that which created us. We have given it the name "God" but it may be easier

---

⁴⁰ *A Course in Miracles*, Foundation for Inner Peace, 1975, page 2.

to comprehend what it is we are aligning with if we think of it as the *Grand Operational Design*.

In ancient times, before the scientists began to theorize and test their beliefs about existence and the structure and operation of the universe, people credited everything they saw and experienced to God's Will. They not only attributed everything to God but gave credit for everything they received to God; thereby, unwittingly, subscribing to the principle of One Will.

At some point in our human evolution we began to believe in a divided will—our will and God's Will. We further exacerbated the division by ascribing the bad things that we saw or experienced as the fault of a negative force that tempted and forced us to make choices that were out of alignment with God's Will. We named this entity "Satan" or "the Devil" who then became the scapegoat for our negative behavior and experiences. Alternately, we gave some credit for our negative experiences to a punishing God who was angry with us for letting Satan tempt us into wrongdoing.

Ultimately, scientists (metaphysicians included) began understanding the dynamics of the energy that forms the basis of everything in existence. We began to realize that there is an orderly design to the Universe that is based on provable laws that act, react and interact with itself and all of creation.

This realization took the biblical meaning of "made in the image and likeness of God" to an entirely different level: We are made in the image and likeness of energy itself, because we are energy.

This may disturb some people who have become more comfortable with the anthropomorphic concept of God; however, let me assure you that this in no way eradicates the personal Father-Mother-type relationship many of us have with our Creator. Our elder brother, Jesus, who was a metaphysician of the first order, referred to God as "Abba" or Father. It was his way of developing a closer walk with that Universal Life Force. The upside of this is that it makes it more personal and easier to relate to; however, the downside is that it can instill within us a greater sense of separation from it. That being said let us continue with our attempts to understand the One Will.

God, then, is the orderly construct of the Universe, operating under, by and through immutable laws, that interacts with its Creations by way of a divinely personal connection. When we understand the laws upon which it is based and align our thoughts, words and choices with those Laws, we are in concert with the One Will. We might even say that we *are* the One Will, which makes sense of the statement in *A Course in Miracles* that "God's Will is my Will."

What happens when we don't align with this Grand Operational Design?

The *Prodigal Son* is a great example of what happens when we are determined to have it "My Way." He had been living a life of privilege, having all of his needs met as the offspring of a very wealthy father, and was unaccustomed to struggle or having to fend for himself. From the scripture we might surmise that he either had never been to the big city or had only done so in the company of his family. It did not occur to him that he was ill-prepared to be on his own and manage a very large sum of money without a plan. From the scripture we might conclude that the eldest brother was the one working beside the father managing the day-to-day operations, which was more than likely the reason for his upset over the situation upon his brother's return. This, however, did not cross the mind of the younger brother in his determination to exercise his *free will*. The greatly predictable outcome was that, in a very short time, his money was gone and so were the people who had sought his company while the money was flowing.

The Bible states that "there was a famine;" however, there is no further indication of why this affected the *Prodigal Son*. It also says "he began to be in want." Metaphysically, *famine* represents "lack of faith in God's power to prosper."[41] To "be in want" means to lack even the most basic needs. So he found himself in a very difficult situation.

The very nature of *need* presupposes that there is something somewhere that can fulfill the need; however, in the case of the *Prodigal Son*, metaphysically representing our immaturity, there is a missing element: a basic understanding of how to connect with what it is we are in need of, much less comprehending the idea of aligning with the *One Will*. What, then, is the key to aligning with the One Will?

When we align with the One Will, we establish a partnership with the Source of all that we need, require and desire. It contains every possibility and the ultimate outcome that assures we will be provided for even in the midst of whatever "famine" may be present in our lives. There is never a doubt or fear because abundance is the natural order of the universe and the universe is governed by the Grand Operational Design—the Source of all good and Creator of all existence. It is an ever-present energy of substance that is ready and waiting to be called into manifestation.

How do we align with this One Will?

We align with the One Will by establishing a connection and maintaining an ongoing relationship with it. While we are made up of It and always one with It, we have been given Free Will and It does not interfere with what It has given us lovingly. It is by our own desire to know this Presence and Power intimately that It is revealed to us. Through daily practice of prayer and meditation, by living in integrity with every other living thing and

---

[41] *The Revealing Word*, Unity School of Christianity, 1959, page 71.

by remembering that we are part and parcel of this Presence, we begin to live under Its guidance and direction.

The key to getting there is awareness. Awareness is focused attention to the details of life—the messages, spiritual meaning and lessons within everything around us and everything that happens to us. By recognizing that everything happens for a reason—happens not to us but for us—we use life as a tool for conscious evolution and the route to home.

The process for getting there is daily practice. How do we get to Carnegie Hall? Practice, Practice, Practice. Practicing a daily activity of prayer, meditation and/or silence will over time become habit and, ultimately, a lifestyle. Once the relationship is established, we can seek and receive guidance and direction for achieving any goal or overcoming any challenge in our lives.

In our Exercises at the end of this chapter, you will be provided with some tools for establishing a daily practice for connecting with the Divine part of you and learning how to hear the Voice for God.

There is a little voice inside that tells us when we are headed in the right direction or when something is not good for us. We avoid many mishaps and much suffering when we listen for and to It.

"My Way" was a great hit for Frank Sinatra but it can be a big "miss" for us. Listen to your inner guidance and avoid the pitfalls of the ego.

EXERCISE

For the next twenty-one (21) days make a commitment to spend 10 minutes in the morning and 10 minutes in the evening in either meditation or the silence with the intention of getting guidance for a particular situation or condition in your life. Each day at the appointed time, find a place that is quiet and where you will not be disturbed, turn off the phones and sit in a comfortable place. Taking several slow, deep breaths, you will relax your body and mind. Do not push; simply allow it to happen. Then focus on your breath as it enters and leaves the tip of your nostrils, using that as a placeholder to come back to when your mind begins to wander. When you feel totally relaxed and centered, ask for guidance on the situation, being willing to do nothing until it is received then, using an idea from A Course in Miracles, ask the following questions:

> What would you have me do?
> Where would you have me go?
> What would you have me say and to whom?[42]

Sit in the silence for approximately five (5) minutes. Listen or feel for that quiet urging (that still small voice) and take note of any images that move across your mind. Take several deep breaths and open your eyes. During the day be watchful for signs, messages or even human intervention that comes in response to your request.

Journal each day.

A PRAYER

Dear God, help me to walk in courage wherever my path may lead me, reminding me that I never walk alone. Lead me, guide, direct me and order my steps that every step I take leads to you.
Amen

---

[42] *A Course in Miracles*, Foundation for Inner Peace, 1975.*[paraphrased]*

AN AFFIRMATION

I will with the Will of God and I am directed in
making right choices and taking right actions that
lead me in the direction of my highest good.

STUDY QUESTIONS:

1. How has your understanding of the Will of God been impacted by this chapter?
2. Have you previously been aligning more with the human will or God's Will?
3. What specific steps would you need to take in your own life to align more with the One Will?
4. Has there ever been a time when you knew that you had decided against God's Will? Why? What happened?
5. How does this stage in the Journey relate to your own life?

IV

ACCEPTING OUR DIVINE PURPOSE

STEP FOUR — Accept Your Assignment—Determine your soul's purpose and begin living from it.

[16]He would gladly have filled himself with the pods that the pigs were eating; and no one gave him anything. [17]But when he came to himself he said, 'How many of my father's hired hands have bread enough and to spare, but here I am dying of hunger! ~ Luke 15: 16-17

He came to himself. . .What does that mean?

He came to the realization that this wasn't it. In a moment of clarity, he realized that his decisions had brought him to the depths of despair. For the first time, there was nothing left but the time to see the path his choices had laid. He was able to reflect, to review the journey, to this point and found it far less than both what he had originally intended. In other words, he woke up and realized he had made a huge mistake.

Or had he?

Everyone comes to themselves at some point in their

lives—maybe more than once—so, here again, this parable hits home, does it not?

The *Prodigal Son* has found himself feeding and eating with the pigs after blowing the entire fortune demanded from his father. But he came to himself! What better time to take this step than at the moment we are assaulted by the stench and image of pigs in their natural habitat? Everyone of us, at some point, has found ourselves surrounded by the stench of our own making, coming to a realization that this was not who we were and how we wanted our lives to look. Suddenly, our eyes are opened and we seem to have a greater clarity—if only to ask ourselves: "How on earth did I wind up here?" The things that were taking our focus were falling apart around us, so there is no need to give that any more energy. We now see the Forest.

For example, if we had been using all of our energy to maintain a job in which we were miserable but, fearing that, to be without that job we would have nothing, we put all of our efforts toward *keeping* that job. One day, after all our efforts, we arrive at work and are immediately fired or laid off. What just happened? What are we to do? At that moment, the job is *behind* us and there is nothing *before* us, so there is only what is right in front of us. There is only that which is *within* us.

Perhaps, we were working against the Universe, in opposition to our *Soul Purpose*. Perhaps, the Universe needed to get our attention and couldn't get a subtler message through the thick walls of our desperation to hold onto that dead-end, miserable, useless job. Sometimes, the cosmic two-by-four or wrecking ball is the most efficient way of getting through.

At times we are too busy putting all of our energy into something that no longer serves us; however, the Soul is always keeping us on track whether we know it or not and will enroll other Souls to play roles in the very drama called for in order to wake us up and get us back on track. Sometimes, like the *Prodigal Son,* we have to lose everything to force us to turn to the Holy Spirit (the Source) for divine guidance. That guidance may come as a two-by-four and our cry for help may merely be: "Why?"

But, as you have discovered from previous chapters, our Spiritual Journey is purposeful and has meaning. The greatest losses, the deepest wounds and the most challenging situations are often what cause us to ask, first, "why?" However, what usually comes next is: "What now?" Rarely do we have the luxury of just lying there waiting to die. Normally, the Divine Spark, from somewhere deep within, sets off an alarm that triggers a will to survive and we "come to ourselves."

H. Emilie Cady says:

> "*Sometime, somewhere, every human being must come to himself. Having tired of eating husks, he will arise and go to my Father.*" ~ Luke 15:18.[43]

Unity teachers, Charles Fillmore and Elizabeth Sand Turner, point out that "coming to oneself" means coming to the awareness of that Divine Spark, which reminds us that we are greater than the situation we find ourselves experiencing. Rev. Jim Lee taught us to say "the power within me is greater than the situation before me." And that is the absolute truth. There is nothing outside of us that can stand up against what is within us.

The *Prodigal Son* has come to himself and has made the decision to go home. He has discovered his place in the universe, has accepted the One Will, has taken responsibility for his part in the situation and has made the decision to go home. Just as both he and Dorothy found the power within them to make the journey

---

[43] *Lessons in Truth,* H. Emily Cady, Unity Books, 1894, page 6.

home, we have the power to return to the Father's House—that place in the heart where we find our home in Spirit (God).

That sounds wonderful and, at first, sounds easy; however, after reflecting on it for a moment, we are left with: "How do I get back? What must I do?"

EXERCISE: Say YES to the Universe!

Say YES to the Universe! The Prodigal Son simply retraced his steps and made the trip home. Dorothy clicked her heels three times and she was home and it had all been a bad dream. For us, because we live simultaneously between two worlds, we have a few more steps:

1. Declare your Willingness: Say YES to the Universe!
2. Become Aware—Pay Attention!
3. Discover your Soul's Purpose
4. Accept your Purpose
5. Live On Purpose

EXERCISE: Paying Attention

While the act of "Paying Attention" is not easy, the process itself is simple. All it requires is that we become alert to everything that is going on around us at every moment, which includes everything the five senses experiences. It means being present to every smell, sound, touch, taste and seeing deeply into what our eyes behold. The challenge is that we must do this while functioning in this world of blatant distractions.

We are continually bombarded with sights, sounds, smells, tastes, etc.; however, we have become so numb to them, we are not really paying attention to them. In other words, we have become so accustomed to them we have drowned them out for the most part and now they are like "white noise." Within every sound, every touch, every taste is a vibration that literally pulsates with life force and connects us with the eternal link to the Creator and Its Creations. By being fully present to all of it, we can only be in this present moment without falling into the trap of experiencing the present moment based on our experiences of the past. When we are successful at this, we see, hear, taste, touch and smell beyond the mundane to the magnitude of Creation itself. We then are aware.

Once aware, we are tuned in to the Presence of Infinite Spirit and the messages and signs become apparent and we are ready to be guided.

EXERCISE: Discovering Your Soul Purpose

I cannot say that I am an expert in the process for "Discovering Our Soul Purpose" but I have studied with some great Master Teachers and delved into some great writings about how to know what we are here to do. From this, I was able to discover my own and receive multiple confirmations that what I had originally perceived as my purpose was simply a stepping stone to my true *Soul Purpose* and through several processes I was led to the real deal. From that, I can share my discoveries as well as connect you with the wisdom of my great teachers.

There are many signs along our life journey that point us in the direction of our purpose. We often miss them because we are not paying attention and are not observant enough to understand what messages they are bringing to us. Add to that the outside influences in our lives that misdirect us toward the purpose others project upon us.

One of the clues that lead to our Soul Purpose is the gifts, talents, skills, hobbies and interests we have and have had throughout our lives. A simple process of taking the time to write down those things you really love doing and those things you seem to have a talent for, can often bring to light your *Soul Purpose.* You will find the exercise at the end of this chapter.

EXERCISE: Accepting Our Purpose

Simply discovering our purpose is not enough. We must then *accept* it.

I would bet you can name at least one person you know who without a doubt has a purpose they are not pursuing for whatever reason. Perhaps, they had to earn a living in order to take care of their family. Perhaps, the idea of stepping out and pursuing their true purpose is too scary. Whatever the reason, I'll bet you are familiar with someone who falls into this category—perhaps, even yourself!

Just for a moment, allow me to offer an alternative concept that arose out of a discussion with my Editor and close girlfriend, Cindy Farris, while discussing a situation in her life. After seeing the amazing transformation in both our lives, from the work we have done, we often ask ourselves: "Why would anyone want to stay in that pain?" We often say "insanity is doing the same thing over and over, expecting to get a different result" and once we come to ourselves we are able to see this tendency and, ultimately, prevent it.

It suddenly dawned on me that there are people who do the same thing over and over "expecting to get the same result." Both Cindy and I have people in our lives that have a "V" for Victim emblazoned upon their forehead. This state of being has become so familiar and comfortable for them, they are unable to let it go. They have pitched a tent in it and have become comfortably ensconced in the pain and suffering. The pain has become their comfort zone.

Often, I will ask coaching clients that resist moving from Victimhood to Empowered: "What's the payoff?" In other words, what are they getting from this state of being that feeds a need within them. Sometimes it is simply a matter of filling a need for attention. Even negative attention can be better than no attention in some cases and, in these instances, it is very difficult for them to see that getting attention in that manner is not worth the pain and suffering required to sustain it; however, when we have only learned to get that result, we will stay there until we learn a better way. Sometimes it takes a stick of dynamite (cancer, major loss, severe trauma) to force us out of that tent.

What prevents us from *accepting* our purpose? I believe, more often than not, it is because we feel we don't have the support to step out so boldly or the resources to sustain us once we do. The voice of that subconscious *Core Negative Belief is* reciting a litany of: "Who are you to think you can do this?" It is a familiar voice, one we have been hearing and following most of our life and we have come to believe it because we have tried and failed many times so it has to be right. To *accept* our purpose would require turning off or drowning out that voice and that can be very difficult and scary.

How do we tear down the self-constructed barriers to create an opening for *accepting* our purpose? We do so by breaking the chains that bind us to the past.

EXERCISE: Breaking the Chains that Bind You

- Take a closer look at what that *Core Negative Belief* is saying. (Listen carefully to the words)
- Reflect back on the first time you ever heard those words and from whom. (Was it a parent, a teacher, a sibling, a friend?)

- Check in with the feelings/emotions that arise around this memory. (Sad, angry, fear, etc.)
- See how it has prevented you from stepping fully into your power time after time. Choose to let it go. Make the choice to forgive the source of the *Core Negative Belief* and break those chains.
- Choose an effective forgiveness method (i.e., Radical Forgiveness, HeartMath or other process). Stick with it until you feel relief/release. Your body will let you know when the forgiveness is complete. (Think about the person/ situation again and see whether the emotions are still present.)

Begin taking ownership of your purpose and take one baby-step at a time stepping into it. If the voice begins the litany, just say "thank you for sharing" and keep moving forward.

Once we "come to ourselves," what Charles Fillmore calls "the upwardly progressive movement of Spirit" takes over and begins guiding us more deliberately toward the purpose for which we have chosen this Journey. We have left the safe haven of our spiritual home and have begun experiencing the ups and downs of life in this human plane, which has catapulted us into an awakening of who we really are in the midst of the pain and suffering, and now we must make our way "home" again.

But returning "home" does not mean we are seeking to escape the human experiences. It means we begin to experience it consciously aware of the Truth of our being. That is the true purpose of the Journey.

I came to myself in 1978 upon being diagnosed with a life-threatening illness and, again, in 2008 with the end of my marriage. My daughter, Sian, came to herself as she came out of a week-long coma following an automobile accident.

So many people tell me how it took something that shook up their lives to get them on track with their Purpose. We are often moving along comfortably in our lives when BAM!!! The big shake-up occurs and we are shifted out of our comfort zone.

I often say when speaking that "I am not here to comfort the disturbed but to disturb the comfortable." Complacency is the death of one's purpose and, when the Soul sees us in that complacent state it shakes us up so we can move forward. Fulfilling our purpose requires forward movement and it cannot occur through complacency.

Contentment is a state of mind that is conducive to inspiration. Complacency is a state of mind that lulls us into a false sense of security.

EXERCISE: Live on Purpose

When we come to ourselves, we suddenly realize we have been inactive and this causes us to take a look at where we are in our lives. This look-see reveals the need to reconnect with our Soul Purpose and to accept that it is the original objective in initiating this Journey. When we are on purpose, our lives flow easily and effortlessly. Doors open where none existed before and paths are laid out before us like the "yellow brick road."

The key to fulfilling our Soul Purpose is to, first; fulfill our Divine Purpose as creations of the Creator. Once we have aligned with that purpose the rest, as they say, is a "piece of cake." I believe *The Course's* explanation of our Divine Purpose puts it forth clearly and succinctly:

> *"I am here only to be truly helpful. I am here to represent Him Who sent me. I do not have to worry about what to say or what to do, because He Who*

sent me will direct me. I am content to be wherever
He wishes, knowing He goes there with me. I will be
healed as I let Him teach me to heal."[44]

When we remember that it is God who sent us and God who will direct us it becomes easier to Live on Purpose. The ego has been silenced and the way is made clear for The Holy Spirit.

A PRAYER

Beloved Presence, as I affirm my willingness to
live out my purpose, lead, guide and direct my
path that I may live consciously what I have come
to be and to do. I am eternally grateful.
And so it is!

AN AFFIRMATION

I AM on purpose each and every moment of each and every day!

STUDY QUESTIONS

1. Talk or write about a time in your life when you "came to yourself." In other words, when you "woke up" to a realization about yourself or about what you were doing or how you were living your life that was like having a glass of ice cold water thrown in your face.
2. What new insights or wisdom came to you about it?
3. What did you discover about yourself and the forward movement of your life?
4. How did things change after this awakening?
5. Did it affect other parts of your life? How?

---

[44] *A Course in Miracles*, Foundation for Inner Peace, 1975.

V

RECOGNIZING OUR CONNECTION TO OTHERS

STEP FIVE — Work for the Greater Good—Live in awareness of your relationship to others and the planet

[18] I will get up and go to my father, and I will say to him, "Father, I have sinned against heaven and before you; [19] I am no longer worthy to be called your son; treat me like one of your hired hands." [20] So he set off and went to his father. But while he was still far off, his father saw him and was filled with compassion; he ran and put his arms around him and kissed him. [21] Then the son said to him, 'Father, I have sinned against heaven and before you; I am no longer worthy to be called your son." ~ Luke 15:18-21

The more we awaken as individuals the more we discover we are <u>not</u> individuals.

Before the *Prodigal Son* left home, he was seeing the world from the limited perspective of the ego or personality—once he broke the ties to the unit (even though that was only in his mind), he became the "I" interacting with other "I-Selves" without the supportive cellular structure of the unit—his actions were then derived from a me-centered belief system that had no regard for or awareness of the consequences upon the collective—when he found himself with the pigs (the dark night of the soul), his I-self was stripped down to nothing (no thing) and he realized (remembered—came to himself) that he was part of something greater and returned home.

He evolved to a higher awareness—he was able to see himself from a higher perspective—the "we-centered" perspective. As in the case of the *Prodigal Son*, we sometimes must lose those things that contribute to our sense of self (ego) in order to gain a sense of Self (Divine Self, The Christ). When there is nothing left but the personality at its lowest point, the desire to understand how we got there often leads to who we truly are.

My friend, Tra Boxer, lost everything in the Oakland fire—her beautiful 5000 square-foot home on top of a hill overlooking a panoramic vista of the Bay. In recounting her experience, she said she realized how blessed she was to be alive and that her husband and children were not harmed. She recognized that the experience has taught her to appreciate her beautiful things but not to idolize or worship them. Now, she enjoys the beauty of her current home and works of art without attachment. What she appreciates more is her joy, health, family and friends.

When I lost everything I owned in 1991, it was a revelation for me that all of those "things" were given to me by a Source that could give me all that back and then some. This was confirmed for me when I moved from Sacramento to Walnut Creek in 2011, from a 3500 square-foot house to much smaller house, and I delighted in giving away 80 percent of the things I had acquired since my loss.

What was important to both Tra and me was that the people we loved were our primary focus, not the things we had. We recognized our connection to others and not the things.

The scripture says "while he was still a long way off. . ." the

Father began preparing to celebrate his return. Even at a great distance, he *knew* his Son. This assures us that we can never be too far away that God will not recognize us. God knows us, because we are a part of God. While we may believe in our own minds, like Dorothy that we have left "the Father's house", that is virtually impossible. Even when we have closed our minds and hearts to God, we are still right there in God.

The most powerful point of this portion of the scripture is that these preparations were being made while he was still quite a distance away. It tells me that the father was *looking* for his son; in fact, one could easily surmise that he had probably made frequent trips to a spot where he could see his son even in the far-off distance. Perhaps, ever since the son left home, the father had been looking for him to return and never gave up believing it would happen.

Wow! As "the father" in this parable represents God, this scripture is telling us that God is always watching for our return and will never give up believing that we *will* find our way home. Additionally, God is so certain of our return that, even when our consciousness is still in the distance, preparations begin for our return—the Red Carpet is rolled out.

This reminds me of an old Unity Affirmation: I am the rich child of a loving parent whose good pleasure is to give me the Kingdom of Heaven."

In other words, our Creator just can't wait to give us all that we could ever need, require or desire and then some. If that is the case, and I do believe it is, all we need is a great desire and a little bit of faith, added to the awareness of our connection to God and the Cosmos.

Recently, my income was reduced by a significant monthly amount. At first, I was very upset with the person who—by not keeping their word—put me in a financial bind just before Christmas. My daughter reminded me that there was no need to worry, because God always takes care of me. Then I remembered that I had said I would be glad when I didn't need the money coming from this source. LOL! Be careful what you affirm. Obviously, God, in Its Infinite Wisdom, decided that I didn't need it anymore. I laughed and stepped out on faith. Wouldn't you know it, money started coming in from other sources.

It appears, then, that from the moment we "come to ourselves," the gates are open and the Kingdom of Heaven is spread out for our arrival. All we need do is *realize* who we are and we are just as good as home.

Once we realize that we are one with the entire universal family of God—the Cosmos—everything is set up for us to live within the Kingdom and enjoy all of God's largesse each and every moment of each and every day.

First, we remember who we are and whose we are; then, we recognize that there is nothing that separates us from God and all of God's creation; and, finally, we begin the inner journey to discover spiritual truths that open the way for our robe, slippers and ring—eternal abundance.

Let me know this brother as I know myself [45].

Charles Fillmore says: "If God is the Father of all, then men and women are brothers and sisters in a universal family, and he who sees spiritually should open his heart and cultivate that inclusive love which God has given as the unifying element in the human family." [46]

Yet, we are so powerfully wired to choose, demonstrate and experience our *Free Will* that we are even afforded the opportunity to have the full experience of our pain and suffering, although we never left home in the first place. It is the highest proof that we were given *dominion* over the things of the earth and God will

---

[45] *A Course in Miracles,* Foundation for Inner Peace, 1975, p 72.

[46] *Christian Healing,* Charles Fillmore, Unity Books, 1909, p 131.

not interfere with the curriculum our Soul has designed for our growth and evolution in consciousness.

Quantum Science has proven beyond any doubt that we are continually interacting and interdependent with each other through an energy link that connects all energy that makes up all life.

As I write this book, I am witnessing extremes in human behavior and in weather patterns. It is no coincidence that as the energy of violence increases throughout the world, there is a corresponding manifestation of violent weather patterns. All life is inextricably linked and the thoughts, words and emotions of these human co-creators are playing out on the big screen of our lives.

> *The study of Truth will either make us more adaptable to situation; more friendly in our relations with others, because we discover the unity of universal brotherhood; or else it will fail in its purpose for a time and cause us to be introverts, given to abnormal introspection, inclined to hold ourselves apart for the world about us.*[47]

It is essential that we live our lives in the awareness of this cosmic cohesiveness in order to work in concert with what we wish to see in the manifest realm. It is, therefore, essential that we recognize that what we do to others we are doing to ourselves. I recently posted on Facebook: "I am you and you are me. How I treat you is how I treat myself. How you treat me is how you treat you. Live life with that in mind and you'll see a great shift in the collective consciousness and a more positive energy manifestation on the planet."

Scripture tells us that there are only two necessary commandments to live by and all the others will take care of themselves:

---

[47] *Mightier Than Circumstances*, Frank B. Whitney, Nabu Press, 2011, p51.

"Love the Lord your God with all your heart and with all your soul and with all your strength and with all your mind; and love your neighbor as yourself."
~ Luke 10:17 NIV

Jesus was responding to a question from one of the disciples who wanted to know which of the commandments was the greatest (most important). He was making the point that we don't have to keep a lot of Commandments if we keep the two basic ones. In other words, loving God and loving our neighbor established a firm foundation for holding fast to the rest of them.

In order to discover our place in the cosmos and our connection to others, we must take each day as if it were a piece of a jigsaw puzzle that makes up the "Spiritual Big Picture". Study it carefully, noting its shape, color, texture and substance to see where it fits in the Universal Scheme of things and how it fits into the Divine Plan. As you go along, it will all make sense as the picture unfolds.

As we witness the situations and circumstances taking place upon our planet, we must take a look at where we are contributing— co-creating—to the energy behind them. For example, if we are seeing *violence* and *conflict* all around us, it is essential that we keep watch for any thoughts, words or emotions that carry the energy of *conflict* and make a shift to our hearts to generate love, peace and compassion in their place.

I recently challenged our congregation and the congregation at Unity Spiritual Center in San Francisco to participate in "A Holiday Without CCJ" (criticism, condemnation, judgment) over a 21-day period of Christmas to New Year's Day. During this time, we would make an effort to catch ourselves before or during the act of criticizing, condemning or judging. If we committed a CCJ, we would put $1 in a jar, box or can and donate the total amount collected to some project at the church. My contribution to Unity of Walnut Creek's music program was $43, an average of two (2) CCJs a day; most of which was collected the first 10 days. After a while, it got easier and easier to catch myself *before* the CCJ.

Once we recognize our connection, it is essential to live *consciously*. What do I mean by that? By living as if we are the *cause behind the effect* at all times and, in fact, we are.

EXERCISE:

1. Sit facing another person or hold a mirror in front of you;
2. Repeat the following (from memory or record it so you can repeat it out loud):
   > I give you to the Holy Spirit as part of myself
   > I acknowledge that you will be released
   > Unless I wish to use you to imprison myself
   > In the name of my freedom I choose your release
   > Because I recognize that we will be released together.[48]

3. Sit quietly, realizing the depths of the statement you have just made.
4. Take a deep breath, exhale and thank your partner or yourself in the mirror.
5. Stand up and hug (you can also hug yourself).

We were given *dominion* over the things of the earth. It does not mean simply taking care of the *physical* things of the planet. It also means taking care of the *spiritual* things of the planet. In other words, taking our role as Co-Creators as seriously as God does. It means taking care of each other.

How might we do this?

---

[48] *A Course in Miracles*, Foundation for Inner Peace, 1975, p 329.

1. Set an intention to live from the heart 24 hours a day;
2. Speak consciously. (Are these words I'd like to see on the 6 o'clock news?)
3. Monitor emotions and pull out of those we don't want to manifest as quickly as possible
4. Send loving energy from the heart to everyone everywhere we go (work, grocery store, mall, etc.)
5. Treat others as you would like to be treated.

If only one or two of these could be maintained, what a wonderful world this would be.

A PRAYER

"The Prayer of St. Francis"

Lord, make me an instrument of thy peace.
Where there is hatred, let me sow love;
Where there is injury, pardon;
Where there is doubt, faith;
Where there is despair, hope;
Where there is darkness, light;
Where there is sadness, joy.

O divine Master, grant that I may not so much seek
To be consoled as to console,
To be understood as to understand,
To be loved as to love;
For it is in giving that we receive;
It is in pardoning that we are pardoned;
It is in dying to self that we are born to eternal life

AN AFFIRMATION

I am open and receptive to the good that awaits me.

STUDY QUESTIONS

1. Have your ever felt truly connect to someone or something? What was that like?
2. How do you feel about your relationship to the world when you see and hear about all the tragedies in the world and acts of violence being committed by some of our brothers and sisters?
3. What if those perpetrators are simply "you making a different choice?"
4. Have you discovered your assignment or soul purpose for this life journey? If so, are you living it?
5. What could you do to make a deeper connection with the universe and humankind?
6. When will you do it?

VI

LIVING THE LAW—THE CHRIST SELF RETURNS

STEP SIX — Live the Law—Awaken the Divine Power within by intentionally working with the Law.

²²But the father said to his slaves, 'Quickly, bring out a robe—the best one—and put it on him; put a ring on his finger and sandals on his feet. ²³And get the fatted calf and kill it, and let us eat and celebrate;'
~ Luke 15:22-23

The long journey [home] culminates right where we are now, with the realization of the Truth of our Being. That is home.

There is an impeccable Divine Plan imprinted upon the Spiritual DNA of our Souls. It does not impede our Free Will, but every longing and seeking compels us to follow its path. It is so insistent upon completion that even our inadvertent or deliberate forays off the path still lead us to its fulfillment. It is our Blueprint for Divine Potential and it must be awakened; it must be realized, if we are to fulfill the purpose for which we took this journey in the second place and for which we exist in the first place: To express our Creator in the manifest realm as unconditional and forgiving love, in other words, to be the Christ.

Let us not allow the word *Christ* to stop us in our tracks. Instead, let us, first, understand what *Christ* means. The word *Christ* comes from the Greek *khristos* meaning "the anointed"; another way of saying this is that we are "chosen". As children of God, this is why we are being so insistently called by this homing signal toward fulfillment. However it is difficult to hear the call to our Christ nature as we are continually in the midst of our never-ending loop of information through the ever expanding field of technology.

Eckhart Tolle says that the noise in our minds—that extremely loud voice of the ego orating the laundry list of our limitations, disabilities and sins—blocks out the still small voice of the real me, the real you, and prevents us from bringing forth that real part of us, which is the divine part of us—what we call *The Christ*. We are always connected to the divine part of us—it is "part" of us; however, the signal is jammed by the congestion of all the traffic inside our minds.

Although it appears impossible to live in alignment with The Christ of our being, it is not only possible to do so, it is the very purpose for which we left home in the first place; to experience what we are not in order to discover who we are. So, what is *The Christ*, how do we discover it and live in alignment with it?

In Revelation 21:1-8, we are given a word picture of the world as it can be when we fulfill the New Heaven on Earth. In verse 3, it describes The Christ:

> *And I heard a loud voice from the throne saying, "Look! God's dwelling place is now among the people, and he will dwell with them. They will be his people, and God himself will be with them and be their God.*
> ~ Rev 21:8 NIV

Here is the message to us that God will no longer be a deity of the sky or spiritual realm, but will actually dwell among us. Dwelling among us means "being part of us" - in other words, being "within" us. When we accept that we are one with God and made in Its image and likeness and when we learn to live in alignment with that realization, the Christ returns and lives among us, which means we *are* The Christ.

The Christ is the Divine Blueprint that was imprinted upon the genetic code of our Souls that holds the plans for becoming the architects of the Kingdom of Heaven to be built upon the earth. It is the true nature of us that never left home and acts as the placeholder for the awakening that occurs when we remember who we are.

There are references to this Divine Blueprint in all of the ancient Wisdom Teachings.

In the Bible, Jesus of Nazareth says:

Know ye not that ye are Gods? ~ John 10:34

The way of discovering *The Christ* is within and the location is through the heart. The heart itself is God and the key to awakening this Greater Self is LOVE. By learning to love ourselves and others, we open the gateway for Love to begin carrying out the Divine Blueprint for our lives and for our world.

But how do we "live the law?" What is the "law?"

Law is the divinely ordered system of universal interaction that both subordinates to our commands and works for our benefit. The Universe is an orderly system of laws. As co-creators with God, we hold in our power the ability to manipulate this Universal Law and have it meet our needs.

The Catch-22 of this, however, is that the Law works whether we consciously work it or not, because whatever we are thinking, feeling, speaking or doing directly impacts the Law and facilitates it operation. The Law is always working. It can, however, work for us or against us. Consciously working with the Law, works to our benefit. Unconsciously working with the law often serves to our detriment.

Law is precise. It cannot be coerced or manipulated.

Metaphysically, Law is *"the faculty of the mind that holds every thought and act strictly to the truth of being regardless of circumstances or environment. Law is a mathematical faculty. It places first things first. Laws of mind are just as exact and undeviating as the laws of mathematics. To recognize this is the starting point in finding God."*[49]

This is because God IS Law.

> *"Man does not make the law. The Law is and it was established for our benefit before the world was formed."*[50]

God and Universe are synonymous. Law is energy acting upon or from a cause and God is Energy.

The Bible says:

> *"God is Spirit, and those who worship him must worship in Spirit and Truth."* ~ John 4:24

Spirit and energy are the same. "The only difference between Christ and presence is that Christ refers to your indwelling divinity regardless of whether you are conscious of it or not, whereas presence means your *awakened* divinity or God-essence."[51] Presence and Spirit are the same.

---

[49] *The Revealing Word*, Charles Fillmore, Unity School of Christianity, 1959.
[50] *The Revealing Word*, Charles Fillmore, Unity School of Christianity, 1959.
[51] *The Power of Now*, Eckhart Tolle, Namaste Publishing, 1999, p 86.

What this says to me is that worship, which is synonymous with abide by or obey, is the act of living in alignment with God's Law or the Law of the Universe. When we live in alignment with Law, we draw into our lives the manifestation of our highest and best—love, joy, peace, prosperity, wholeness—and when we are living a life of love, joy, peace, prosperity and wholeness, we are living in the Kingdom of Heaven which, after all is the ultimate goal.

When the Prodigal Son gets home, he is embraced by the Father and given new slippers, a beautiful robe and a ring. These are the physical out-picturing of the good that awaits us when we get to the Kingdom of Heaven.

In a present-day scenario, these manifestations might appear as happiness, loving family and friends, a great career that we truly love, a wonderful spiritual community of like-minded people and every need being met. It might manifest as a healing from a life-threatening illness. It might mean the healing of a fractured relationship between loved ones. It will manifest as an individualized expression of the desires of our heart.

A PRAYER

Let your light, Oh Christ of my Being, shine through me, that I may experience and express you in all that I say, think and do. Live in me, Live through me, Live as Me moment by moment. Amen

AN AFFIRMATION

I am poised and centered in the Christ Consciousness; nothing can disturb the calm peace of my Soul.

STUDY QUESTIONS:

1. How can you recognize when you are living the Law?
2. Reflect on a time when you knew you were totally out of alignment with Law.
3. Reflect on a time when you felt you were fully in alignment with the Law.
4. Does seeing yourself as The Christ cause any discomfort or does it feel natural? Why?
5. What would this world look/feel like if we all recognized each other as the Christ?
6. Practice saying: "I am (your name) the Christ."

VII

CREATING HARMONY IN OUR WORLD — THE POWER OF FORGIVENESS

STEP SEVEN — Keep the Peace — Contribute consciously and creatively toward peace and harmony in the world through Forgiveness.

"...²⁴for this son of mine was dead and is alive again; he was lost and is found!' And they began to celebrate. ~ Luke15: 24

Wow! What a homecoming that was. I can imagine Dorothy's homecoming was just as amazing, even if the Journey had only been in her mind. Auntie Em would have prepared all of her favorite foods and she would have received special treatment.

But, putting aside the robe, slippers, ring and feast for a moment, there is a deeper significance to this Homecoming than initially meets the eye.

The *Prodigal Son,* before leaving home, demanded his inheritance and left of his own accord to go out into the world and "find himself." He defied family traditions, left his Father and Brother with all of the responsibilities of what appears to have been a rather large estate and went off to make his own way in the world. Then, to add insult to injury, he blew the entire inheritance and came back penniless.

To give him credit, however, he knew he had messed up and was willing to return as a hired hand and work for his room and board. He did not return in arrogance. But, let's look more deeply into this homecoming to uncover a secondary Teach Point within Jesus' story.

This is a story of the ultimate demonstration of *Forgiveness*. Although it begins as an example of how we often wind up experiencing pain and suffering as a result of our need to experience life, find ourselves and evolve in consciousness as our challenges push us to a point where we awaken and "come to ourselves," it offers a second major Teach Point: How our Father, God, views our transgressions.

In *A Course in Miracles* it tells us that there is nothing to forgive because nothing wrong happened in the first place. This is also the foundation principle of Colin Tipping's *Radical Forgiveness* process.

To truly understand how this level of forgiveness works, let's look at Tipping's Five (Stages) of Forgiveness and how they correlate with the point of this story. The Five (5) Stages are:

1. Tell the Story
2. Feel the Feelings
3. Collapse the Story
4. Reframe the Story
5. Integration

TELL THE STORY:

In this first Stage, we tell our story from the victim's viewpoint. This naturally follows the story of the *Prodigal Son*, as his story begins with leaving home with his inheritance to prove he could make it on his own and, subsequently, his immaturity, selfishness, greed and pigheadedness (couldn't resist the pun) sent him spiraling into pain and suffering. He was a victim of his own ego.

FEEL THE FEELINGS:

As we know, he ended up wastefully spending all of his inheritance on strangers pretending to be his friends until the money was gone. From the description of his circumstances, it is a good bet that he experienced feelings and emotions of regret, fear, self-loathing, shame, self-recrimination and disgust. In his own words, he tells us: *16 He would gladly have filled himself with the pods that the pigs were eating; and no one gave him anything (Luke15:16).* I think it's pretty clear what he was feeling.

COLLAPSE THE STORY:

This step entails looking at the story, removing what we made up about it and leaving "just the facts" as Detective Friday of Dragnet used to say. When we collapse the story of the Prodigal Son, we are left with: He demanded his inheritance; spent it all; was left destitute; and had to go back home.

REFRAMING THE STORY:

In this step, we look at the story for the gifts it brought, what we learned or how we grew spiritually as a result. When the Prodigal Son "came to himself," he realized his journey was to show him that he had a loving father, who would welcome him home and give him the riches of his estate and forgive him all his transgressions. In fact, his father would never hold it against him in the first place. His experience was simply an opportunity to discover how blessed he was. This is, by far, the most important of all the stages. This is where we determine the value of the experience. This is what empowers us. We cannot be a victim and experience our power at the same time. This stage frees us from the burden blame places upon us.

INTEGRATION:

In this step we take some type of action that integrates what we've learned through our forgiveness work and integrate it at a cellular level, so that it becomes part of us. In the case of the Prodigal Son, I believe his journey back home was an act of Integration. In Radical Forgiveness workshops or coaching, we do breath-work or dance or do cushion work as a form of Integration; it is some type of movement that sends a message to the entire cellular family of the body that we have taken this process in at a cellular level.

We can see, from these Stages of Forgiveness that the entire experience of the *Prodigal Son* was purposeful and had meaning. It becomes clear, also, that this was a Journey of the Soul that facilitated spiritual growth—an elevation in consciousness.

If we look closely, we see how the roles of the three protagonists of our story all play a vital part in not only fulfilling the Soul Purpose of the *Prodigal Son*, but also the fulfillment of the Soul Contract agreed to by the Father and the Other Son as well. Jesus was simply trying to make a point about forgiveness, restoration and love with this Parable and the others he strung together in his sermon that day.

I refer to all three of the characters in this story as "protagonists" because each plays a major role in helping Jesus get to this Teach Point. Each, in their own way, was critical to the unfolding of this ultimate demonstration of unconditional love and forgiveness.

The *Prodigal Son* (the younger son) is a case study for several things: selfishness; immaturity; reckless behavior; impatience and pigheadedness (couldn't resist the pun). The Core Negative Beliefs that motivated his actions were: "No one takes me seriously" and "My father likes my brother better than me." The decision was: "My father is old and out of touch; I'm not going to be like my father."

Can any of you see yourself in this character? I can. I was so sheltered as an "only child" that I couldn't wait to be free from the oppression of my parents. My first date was senior prom and my second date was graduation night. When I finally got to college I went wild; however, I didn't know how to handle the freedom. Even though I was in a women's college, we were quickly schooled by our big sisters in the art of rule-breaking. This curriculum included: sneaking out of the dorm; having our dorm-mates support us in sneaking back in; and other techniques for beating the system. If I'd had even a small glimpse of the ultimate outcome of my actions at that time, I would have studied the art of following the rules.

Would that have been better? Maybe. Maybe not.

The *Other Son* was a case study for several things as well: self-righteousness; fear; jealousy and CCJ (criticism, condemnation and judgment). His Core Negative Beliefs were "My brother was always father's favorite, " "No matter how hard I try, it is never enough" and "I am always last or left out." His decision was: "My brother gets away with murder. I'll never forgive him."

Can any of you relate to that one? Were you the oldest and much was expected of you, but your younger siblings were allowed to get away with things that were acceptable or overlooked in those of a younger stage in their lives? If you had been able to glimpse the future, would you have behaved less perfectly, taken more risks or broken more rules?

Would that have been better? Maybe. Maybe not.

The *Father* was a case study in unconditional love. He had no Core Negative Beliefs. His decision was: "No matter what, you can always come home."

Could this be where we want to be in our lives? I know that this is what I am continually working toward. It is one of the major goals in my life—to love all equally and unconditionally without criticism, condemnation or judgment—and it is truly a moment by moment exercise that is easier at times and very difficult at others. What if this journey, and all of the experiences we encounter and mistakes that we make, are exactly what leads to "happily ever after?"

As you saw in the story of the Taoist Farmer, in an earlier chapter, each incident appeared either good or bad to those who were witnessing his experiences; however, he remained neutral, accepting each as it came without judgment. He appeared content in his willingness to allow his life to unfold in just the way that it happened. In other words, he was simply saying "it is what it is."

What this story teaches us is that feelings/emotions and ultimate actions (or reactions) are based on how we see a situation. It is based on our *perception.* Our perceptions determine our experience. For example, if we perceive a situation as a negative one, our experience will follow that same direction. We will walk away with having had a negative experience. If, of course, we perceive a situation as positive, our experience will follow in kind.

Our perceptions are based on meanings we have attached to certain things, past experiences and Core Negative Beliefs. For example, if we are walking along a path in the woods and come across a long dark thing lying across the road, the mind begins to form a conclusion.

If, for example, we perceive "snake" and we have a fear of snakes, the brain will send the message of "fear" down to the cells of the body that will then transmit the signal to every organ of the body. Our stomach may tighten, the heart might race, the muscles may tense and we might even begin to sweat. Even if we then approach the object and determine it is merely a long stick, we have already had the experience of "snake."

That is how experiences within our lives take us on a roller coaster of emotions and impact our bodies in various ways that may cause physical ailments over a period of time from repeatedly carrying erroneous perceptions.

Perception is based on several things:

1. Interpretation
2. Experiences
3. Feelings and emotions
4. Core Negative Beliefs
5. Unhealed hurts

INTERPRETATION:

Perception reflects how we "see" a situation. In other words, how we "interpret" the situation. If you perceive a situation as "fearful" and that perception then impresses itself upon the amygdala of the brain, which then sends a signal to the 150 trillion cells in the body, which then transmits a signal to the organs of the body. The body then responds to the signal and the heart races, the muscles tighten and blood rushes to the head, creating a physical reaction. The entire body system is engaged.

A good example of this is an analogy often used of encountering a long dark, but indistinguishable object on a path in front of us. When our perception reads "snake" and we have a fearful association about snakes, the scenario above will occur. If there is no fearful association with snakes, the experience will be totally different. We can then pick up the stick and continue happily carefree on our journey.

Interpretation is the trigger that facilitates the response that determines our experience. The *Other Son* interpreted his brother's return as an event that would cause him to be displaced. He had been reveling in his father's praise and having his father all to himself and that which he feared had come upon him. His brother had come back. Now he would no longer be the favorite.

EXPERIENCE:

Our stored memory of previous experiences is another thing that shapes our perceptions. Past experiences are stored within the brain's memory bank and hardwired to cellular memory, which is stored in the outer layer of the body's cells. When we see, hear, taste, touch, smell something familiar, we connect with the experience of that prior experience and it becomes our current experience. The *Prodigal Son's* experience of a comfortable and lavish life in comparison to where he was in the midst of feeding the pigs caused him to "come to himself" and return home.

FEELINGS AND EMOTIONS:

Reoccurrences of feelings or emotions from the past in the midst of a situation can also shape our perception. In the scenario of the "long dark object on the path," the "fear" of snakes shaped our perception, as was the case with both sons. The younger being afraid his father would be angry and not take him back; the older being that his brother would usurp his position.

CORE NEGATIVE BELIEFS:

These are belief that have been born of past experiences that provoked an idea about ourselves or how we were viewed by others and that continued to draw to us similar experiences in order to heal those beliefs. If we hold a Core Negative Belief that we are unworthy or unlovable, we will perceive only that, no matter what is actually occurring.

UNHEALED HURTS:

Here lies the silent killer of authentic perception. The unhealed hurts we carry around prompt us to perceive danger and attacks around every corner. They inspire mistrust and suspicion of the actions and words of others; particularly, those who remind us of the perpetrators of our hurts. This architect of our perceptions may be the most difficult to move beyond, because it requires an act of forgiveness to open the way to shift our perception and requires us to actually shift our perception to support the process of forgiveness.

In fact, all of these things that shape our perceptions about life, people, experiences and ourselves require forgiveness work. Each holds the opportunity to forgive others or to forgive ourselves. When we have forgiven the things that promote erroneous perception, we step into authentic perception and begin to live life seeing things as they really are. When we begin to see things as they really are, we can say and feel that everything is perfect or, at least, be willing to see the perfection in everything.

When we, like the *Prodigal Son* "come to ourselves" are able to see that our lives are of our own making and that the power to actually create the life we wish to live into, we begin to understand the concept of *dominion* over our lives and are empowered to choose peace or pain at each juncture of our lives.

When we are able to see the perfection in everything and everyone (including ourselves) exactly as it is in this moment, we are able to live in harmony with the universe and each other. We cease judging ourselves and others and take responsibility for shifting our perception to see the perfection.

"...what we attack or judge in another is what we hate about ourselves...."[52] (If we didn't have a working knowledge of it within ourselves, we would not recognize it in others. As Tipping says: "if you spot it, you got it. It's you in the mirror."

How do we do this?

1. By looking at everything as a possibility for spiritual growth and evolution in consciousness.
2. By finding the gift in everything that occurs in our lives. If we look for it, we will always find that there was something within every situation that made us just a little bit better or stronger or wiser. Finding the gift removes the stinger and helps us heal and move forward.
3. By forgiving the person or situation, remembering that it is the gift we give ourselves. It is not for the other person; it is for us.
4. By observing our perceptions and studying them to see if they are based on what is actually happening or on one of the architects.

"Happily ever after" is a choice that must be made not once but moment by moment. It is the Father's House. It is the Kingdom of Heaven our elder brother Jesus was trying to describe and support us in having by offering the analogy of the *Parable of the Prodigal Son.*

EXERCISE:

1. Sit quietly with eyes closed.
2. Think of a person or situation in your life that still causes you some emotional pain

---

[52] *Radical Forgiveness*, Colin Tipping, 13 Global Publications, 1997, p 79.

3. Bring to mind exactly what happened. Remember in vivid detail, allowing whatever emotions arise to flow freely

4. Say to them in your mind: I forgive you and release you from the bondage in which I have held both of us. I offer you freedom and I offer myself the freedom I have withheld from you. We are both free to be the Perfect Souls we were meant to be.

5. Take a deep breath. Exhale. Open your eyes.

6. Feel free to repeat this exercise if you still feel the same emotions.

A PRAYER

God, give us grace to accept with serenity
the things that cannot be changed,
Courage to change the things
which should be changed,
and the Wisdom to distinguish
the one from the other.

Living one day at a time,
Enjoying one moment at a time,
Accepting hardship as a pathway to peace,
Taking, as Jesus did,
This sinful world as it is,
Not as I would have it,
Trusting that You will make all things right,
If I surrender to Your will,
So that I may be reasonably happy in this life,
And supremely happy with You forever in the next.
Amen.[53]

---

[53] "The Serenity Prayer", Reinhold Niebuhr (1892 – 1971).

AN AFFIRMATION

I see through the eyes of love and my perception is perfection.

STUDY QUESTIONS:

1. What would "happily ever after" look like for you? (Describe it in writing)
2. From what you have taken away from our journey with the *Prodigal Son,* what would it take to make it possible? What might be preventing it from manifesting?
3. What are you willing to give in order to have it? What are you willing to give up in order to have it?
4. Are you able to see instances in your life where you perceive something or someone in a certain way that turned out to be erroneous? (Describe it in writing)
5. What feelings/emotions did you have following your original perception? What feelings/emotions arose later?
6. What Core Negative Beliefs may have created the original perception? Where did they come from? (Write about it)
7. Are you willing to monitor your perceptions and release your criticisms, condemnations and judgments in order to live "happily ever after?

VIII

AND THE OTHER BROTHER?

²⁵"Now his elder son was in the field; and when he came and approached the house, he heard music and dancing. ²⁶He called one of the slaves and asked what was going on. ²⁷He replied, 'Your brother has come, and your father has killed the fatted calf, because he has got him back safe and sound.' ²⁸Then he became angry and refused to go in. His father came out and began to plead with him. ²⁹But he answered his father, 'Listen! For all these years I have been working like a slave for you, and I have never disobeyed your command; yet you have never given me even a young goat so that I might celebrate with my friends. ³⁰But when this son of yours came back, who has devoured your property with prostitutes, you killed the fatted calf for him!' ³¹The the father said to him, 'Son, you are always with me, and all that is mine is yours. ³²But we had to celebrate and rejoice, because this brother of yours was dead and has come to life; he was lost and has been found." ~ Luke 15: 25-32

What about the Other Son?

Whenever someone writes or speaks about this Parable, they rarely go beyond the brief mention of the "Other Brother" who stayed at home and worked tirelessly beside the Father to keep the estate running smoothly and providing for the future of the family. We merely get an indication that he was jealous or resentful of the reception his younger brother received upon his return, stating:

> *[29]"But he answered his father, 'Listen! For all these years I have been working like a slave for you, and I have never disobeyed your command; yet you have never given me even a young goat so that I might celebrate with my friends."* ~ Luke15:29

We know what he was thinking but what was he feeling?

From the scripture we can probably make some assumptions. His view of the world comes from a place of sense consciousness, where his only perspective of the world is through his own eyes and his own filters. He's worked hard for his father, and never asked for a thing in return. He probably had some criticism, condemnation and/or judgment running through his mind and, possibly, some feelings of anger and jealousy. Perhaps he felt wronged. Maybe even a bit vindictive. The scripture goes no further, because Jesus was making a point. Although the foundation premise of this Parable is "redemption," underlying the story is the forgiving love of the Father. Even though his younger son had taken his inheritance, blown it and returned home reduced to nothing, he was loved and welcomed home. He did not forgive him because he did not hold it against him in the first place.

The "Other Son" represents that part of us, which believes that when others receive, our good is reduced. It is also a part of us that cannot let go of the wrongs others have done and feels they should be punished and not forgiven. This is the part of us that makes difficult our letting go of the past. It keeps us in bondage to the past and to others whom we feel have wronged us in some way and we cannot let them off the hook. I once heard someone say "you have to be in prison to be the jailer." That is so true. We are carrying around every person and situation we have not forgiven. When I speak on forgiveness, I usually have several pieces of luggage pre-set on the stage and pick them up one by one, carrying them around while speaking, to demonstrate how we burden ourselves by unforgiveness.

In every life there are experiences that cause us to feel angry, disappointed, fearful, sad, abandoned, disappointed and other emotions resulting from these experiences. When the brain experiences something that triggers an emotion, it emits an energetic signal. In our bodies are 150 trillion cells, each of which has an outer covering that acts as a receiving/transmitting device and is considered the "mind" of the cell. When the brain experiences something that causes a disturbance, it transmits a signal and the signal is received by every cell, which then transmits a signal to the other cells and to every organ in the body. The emotion is imprinted upon the mind of every cell. Thus, a community experience is initiated.

For example, the brain experiences a life situation that triggers "anger." That emotion of "anger" is transmitted to and imprinted upon every cell and the cells transmit the "anger" to every organ. The body system then begins a symbiotic experience of "anger" among the community. The subconscious mind then correlates that experience of "anger" with every other experience of "anger" one has had and those experienced by the Soul as well. That is why many times we "overreact" to certain experiences. It has nothing to do with what is happening right now, but with what had happened in the past as well the present, and the "anger" is exacerbated.

In an online article in Better Health about "Anger" it says:

"Anger is a powerful emotion. Uncontrolled anger may cause increased anxiety, high blood pressure and headaches, and trigger fights or abuse."[54]

Anger triggers the body's 'fight or flight' response. Other emotions that trigger this response include fear, excitement and anxiety. The adrenal glands flood the body with stress hormones, such as adrenaline and cortisol. The brain shunts blood away from the gut and towards the muscles, in preparation for physical exertion. Heart rate, blood pressure and respiration increase, the body temperature rises and the skin perspires. The mind is sharpened and focused.

The article lists other health issues that may be precipitated by "anger": headaches; digestion problems, such as abdominal pain; insomnia; increased anxiety; depression; high blood pressure; skin problems, such as eczema; heart attack; and strokes.[55]

Over a period of time the emotional impact of our unforgiven experiences take on a life of their own and along with the energy of the Core Negative Beliefs of the subconscious mind draw to us more experiences that parallel the old ones in order to provide us with opportunities to forgive and support our Soul in working through its life path purpose and freeing us from the redundant experiences.

We might surmise that unless the "other brother" chose to emulate his Father's example, and to move to that state of forgiveness, that he might remain in a state that was rooted in sense consciousness…only seeing what his eyes could see and what he could experience. This is what can happen for us if we

---

[54] http://www.betterhealth.vic.gov.au/bhcv2/bhcarticles.nsf/pages/Anger_how_it_affects_people

[55] http://www.betterhealth.vic.gov.au/bhcv2/bhcarticles.nsf/pages/Anger_how_it_affects_people

do not choose forgiveness. For forgiveness is not for others, but for ourselves.

"We had to celebrate and rejoice" - that is the way of God's Forgiving Love. God does not forgive us because God never holds it against us in the first place. Seeking God's forgiveness is somewhat redundant.

As mentioned earlier, the "Father" in this Parable represents "God" and our relationship with God. Naturally, when we return home, God's welcoming love embraces us without question or need for explanation or apology. In fact, we only left home in our minds, for it is impossible to leave Home. It is said that "home is where the heart is" and we never leave our hearts behind. We simply take our focus in the direction of the mind rather than the heart. We focus on things outside of us rather than on the things within us. We live in the world rather than in God. In fact, if we were to take this to another level, we might actually say that "the heart is where home is." When we are in our hearts, we are at home. When we leave the realization of this Truth, like Dorothy, we can click our heels three times—We can connect with the heart and align all three levels of our being: Mind, Body and Spirit. When that alignment is complete, we feel the joyous reunion of our hearts with God's heart and we are embodied within the loving comfort of Home.

Now we don't know if the older brother "came to himself" and forgave his younger brother; however, the actions of the Father are the pivotal piece in this story. Even before the son arrives at the house, and while he was still far away but close enough to see that his arrival was imminent, the Father began to prepare for a noteworthy homecoming for his son. He was simply happy that his son was alive and well and home. That is why it is not necessary to seek God's forgiveness; he has prepared for our homecoming even before we arrive. Home awaits us at the core of our heart and God stands ready to embrace us and give us a Royal welcome.

My daughter, in her rebellious and mindless teenage years, had heaped so much hurt upon me and the household, stealing and totaling my car, taking money, staying away for days at a time at a very young age, hanging out in dangerous places and much more. She finally ran away from home at age 16 and began living a dangerous life; however, when she came out of the coma following the accident that brought her back home for good, I was just overwhelmingly happy that she was alive and able to come home. All that she had done flew out of the window and all I could see and feel was the love for my baby girl. The past disappeared and no longer mattered. She was forgiven and had not even asked.

Why forgive?

Because it provides us with a freedom and peace of mind to be able to create the life we wish to have. It leaves us open for the effortless flow of our good. It creates the space for joy to enter and allows serenity to settle upon us.

My favorite reason to forgive is one from the author and creator of the powerful "Radical Forgiveness Process", Colin Tipping, who says "it is no longer an option; it is our destiny."[56] In other words, as I see it, we are here to forgive.

As Souls, it is our destiny to work out our soul stuff, heal our Core Negative Beliefs and release any residual debilitating energy connected to the life lessons we are here to learn in order to facilitate our evolution in consciousness and balance karmic debt. Once we realize that everything we experience is purposeful and has meaning to the Soul, we can let everything go except the incredible transformation that occurs when we "come to ourselves." In other words, when we realize what this is all about. When we discover life is not a destination but a journey.

---

[56] *Radical Forgiveness*, Colin Tipping, 13 Global Publications, 1997.

If we believe our Souls are eternal, have lived before and will live again and again, then we can easily make the connection that one of the things our Souls have to work out is forgiveness.

I know it sounds like a lot but, simply put what we hold in mind produces after its kind and we are doomed to repeat it until we release it. Forgiveness is the release valve. It is also the gift we give ourselves, as it is not designed to let someone off the hook. It is designed to let *us* off the hook. Forgive and be free.

> *Jan participated in one of my forgiveness workshops. In it, she forgave her stepson, with whom she had experienced many challenges. A week after forgiving him, she received a delivery of flowers. In her note to me she said, "This is truly a miracle because he has never done anything like that in the 30+ years he has been in my life."*

How do we get to that place of forgiveness? And what about those things that are unforgiveable?

First, nothing is "unforgiveable" because, as I mentioned above, forgiveness is the gift we give ourselves. It is a process we undertake in order to relieve ourselves of the burden of carrying around with us the baggage of old hurts, past experiences and debilitating emotions.

Whenever I speak or present a forgiveness workshop and introduce people to the value of forgiveness, I always get the "what-abouts." What about the innocent child who. . .? What about woman who was. . .? What about the man who. . .? Trust me, those questions never fail to arise.

My normal first response is "we are spiritual beings, having a spiritual experience on a human plane in a body" and if our experiences are "spiritual" then even those things that appear very terrible are also "spiritual" and are part of the path toward fulfilling our Soul Purpose. Each experience provides us with opportunities for growth and spiritual awareness that leads us toward understanding that we are here and what this is really about so we can live in alignment with that Reality where we are no longer victims but Co-Creators of our Destiny.

Getting to that place of forgiveness successfully requires a process that guides us step by step. Who we were, and the actions and experiences created by who we were being, is only significant to the degree it served as a springboard to the evolution in consciousness required to propel us forward toward fulfilling the curriculum of our Soul for its evolution in consciousness for this incarnation. We are not our past; we are our present. The only gift the past offers is the learning outcome it provided. When we continually refer back to our, or someone else's, past behavior as a criteria for how we interact with them now, we lose the power of what this moment offers.

The Other Brother represents our inability to let go of the past. It is that deep, unyielding morality that keeps our past actions in front of us and prevents us from forgiving them so we can embrace the learning opportunities they provided with gratitude for who we are now.

In self-forgiveness work, the Other Brother represents the Judging Self that stands at the door of our dreams, desires and progress watching for any movement toward breaking the chains that bind us to the past, weighing it against our core negative beliefs, and alerting the Sabotaging Self that we do not deserve to move forward and must be stopped now. The Sabotaging Self then takes over and stops us in our tracks.

The key to cutting down the past that hangs over our heads is complete forgiveness of us and others. We all make mistakes. Mistakes are the way we learn what and what not to do. Just as a baby has no concept of "hot" until it touches something hot, we have no concept of what is for our highest and best until we experience what is not.

While forgiveness of others is difficult, forgiveness of self holds a higher level of difficulty. We experience confusion as to who is forgiving and who is being forgiven. In his book on Self-Forgiveness, Colin Tipping says:

> *"The term forgiveness implies that there has to be one who forgives as well as the one being forgiven. It requires the subject (the forgiver) and an object (the forgiven) for it to make logical sense. When we forgive others, the condition is met, so there's no problem, but not so with self-forgiveness."*[57]

In self-forgiveness, the interaction is between the Authentic Self and one of the aspects of Self we have denied, disowned or repressed. In forgiving others, the intention is healing or reconciliation. In self-forgiveness, the intention is wholeness.

In truth, with either form of forgiveness, the intended outcome is always wholeness. We cannot be whole when we are holding something against another. There is only one of us; we are *merely* different aspects of that one.

When the Father says, "your brother was lost but now is found; was dead but now lives," he is saying "a part of you was lost and now is found." He was, metaphysically, implying that part of us was dead to us but now has been quickened and now lives.

When we live our lives carrying unforgiveness within us, we constantly draw to us similar experiences as the one we are holding against another or ourselves, to give us an opportunity to

---

[57] *Radical Self-Forgiveness*, Colin Tipping, Sounds True, Inc., 2011.

recognize what is unforgiven and take the necessary steps to do the forgiveness.

My sister-by-another-mother, Brenda, used to get so angry when someone jumped in front of her on the freeway and cut her off. She would yell and curse at them and be tense and upset. (You can imagine how often this occurred in a place like California.) After several years of not only doing her forgiveness work in workshops and coaching but also assisting me with workshops, she was driving from work to home one day when someone did the usual California Do-Si-Do. This time, however, as she was about to react she caught herself and realized why this upset her so much. She remembered all the way back to kindergarten, when kids would jump in front of her in the lunch line and dare her to say or do anything about it. This continued even up until high school. It had made her feel less-than, unimportant, insignificant and helpless. The realization of this and the forgiveness (in her heart and mind) of the people who had done that to her, removed any desire to react to the driver that day. She got it and she was free.

You see, these drivers kept showing up to help her get to her forgiveness of the past so that she could be free right now and create wholeness.

That is why Colin Tipping says:

> *We are not the victims of random acts of good luck or bad luck, or being in the right place at the right time or the wrong place at the wrong time. Our lives are purposeful and have meaning.*[58]

Everything that shows up in our lives has a purpose and a meaning for us along this evolution in consciousness—this journey

---

[58] *Radical Forgiveness*, Colin Tipping, 13 Global Publications, 1997.

home. This journey is one from the head to the heart. It is about living our lives in a way that empowers us to recognize, accept and fulfill our purpose for taking this journey in the first place.

When we are successful at this, our lives take on a new meaning—supporting others in their journey—and a new insights are awakened that expand our purpose to encompass all of humanity.

You see, the Other Brother also represents the sum total of humankind in our universal brotherhood. When we let go of the things that separate us, remove our erroneous perceptions about each other and forgive the hurts we have perpetrated against one another, we see more clearly that which makes us one. When we come to ourselves and recapture the feeling of oneness with God and recognize that our brother is us, we become whole as a species and the world returns to the way it was before the world was.

A PRAYER

Help me to love and forgive my brother as myself; to give up being right to be happy; and to accept all of my brothers and sisters as myself. Teach me to love as you love.
Amen

AN AFFIRMATION

I am the keeper of my brother's freedom and mine.

STUDY QUESTIONS:

1. Have you ever held something against someone long after the situation held any real significance? How did it cause you to feel?

2. Have you noticed any things, small or big, that you hold against people you don't know or with whom you don't really have a relationship?

3. Is there anything you might be holding against yourself? How long have you held this against yourself? Are you willing to let it go?

4. Is there anything in the actions of the Other Brother that remind you of a situation in your own life?

5. What can you do to see humankind truly as your brothers and sisters—as one with you?

IX

AND THEY LIVED HAPPILY EVER AFTER. . .

Is There Life After the Journey or What's Next?

Whew! The journey has come to an end. . .or has it? Is there a journey after "The Journey?" What happens next?

We have no way of knowing exactly what happened to The Prodigal Son once he had completed his journey and returned home; however, if the warm, loving welcome by his Father is any indication, we might surmise that he "lived happily ever after." What else could possibly happen when, as *A Course in Miracles* says: "the condition of love is met?

As spiritual beings having a spiritual experience on a human plane in a body, when does our Journey end?

Is the Journey over when:

1. We come to the realization that we are the creative expressions of that which created us—God?
2. We feel our connection to all life?
3. We have found and fulfilled our Soul's purpose?
4. We have healed all the wounds, forgiven everything and are at peace within ourselves and with the process of life?

Or, is the Journey over when the Soul leaves the physical body and we review our life in retrospect?

Like The Prodigal Son's journey, we also have no concrete idea about what happens after we complete this bodily journey. We can only make an educated guess, based upon near-death accounts and random insights and experiences connected to past lives, that there is something more than this. Based, simply, on the new discoveries in the study of energy, we certainly know that we are energy and that energy is eternal.

But this story has another purpose. This story was used as a Teach-Point. A Teach-Point is technically termed Teaching Point and is that concept or example or idea that brings a story home. It is, as my friend Cindy Farris says, "a nugget" that brings all the students in the room to a mutual understanding.

Jesus, who learned the Essenic Teachings of Judaism from his Mother, Mary, and the traditional teachings of Judaism, along with other universal wisdom from various other Master Teachers along the way, in a sense understood the concept of Student Engagement. He knew that what he learned was critical to a greater understanding of God, our relationship to It and how the Universe works to support us with our every choice. He also knew that our choice determines our experience and had the deep desire to bring these concepts to the masses that they might be released from the cycle of pain and suffering. He also knew, however, that he had to present it at the level of their understanding.

In the principles of teaching, Student Engagement is the process of determining how to support a student in being engaged enough in the value of what is being taught that he or she begins to be "engaged" in the curriculum for personal benefit. It is the switch that engages receptivity to what is being taught.

Jesus understood this concept, even though he knew nothing of student engagement. He simply realized that you had to meet them right where they were; therefore, when he spoke to fishermen, he compared the spiritual principle he was teaching to fish or fishing. When he spoke to farmers, he used the analogy of seeds, sowing, reaping and harvesting. He used Parables.

The Teach-Point of the Parable of the Prodigal Son was designed to bring together people, seekers, of all walks of life into a mutual understanding that:

1. There is no lesser in the Kingdom of God;
2. All of us are the beloved of God;
3. All that God has is ours; and
4. God doesn't have to forgive, because God never holds our mistakes against us in the first place.

The Student Engagement was the forgiving love of the Father and the abundance that was poured out upon him when he returned home. He was teaching that this is how God works on our behalf.

A woman named Megan, whom I met on an Amtrak train, said the line in the scripture that says "and when he was still far away, he saw his son. . ." lets us know that it was not the first time the father had been looking for his son. He may have even gone looking out over the horizon every day, hoping he would return home.

In 1975, my son returned home; however, his was not a journey taken of his own volition; it was a journey I, in the midst of a painful experience, made on his behalf. I gave him up for adoption.

I moved on with my life, but I never moved away from him. I never really felt whole again until that moment when I heard his voice for the first time and then in that moment my eyes fell upon his face for the first time since I had held him in my arms. I never forgot the feel of him in my arms until the moment I held him again and new feelings emerged.

I was born again. I was free. I could be truly free as I never could before. I was no longer searching to fill that that emptiness with something outside of me. I had him again and everything was going to be alright. The guilt was gone. He was handsome, brilliant, successful, talented, and he looked just like his sister and brother. We are so close and we have so much in common and we laugh and talk and enjoy each other tremendously.

Some years later, he blessed us with a wonderful daughter-in-law, Kristan, and, a few years after that, a beautiful granddaughter, Shelby. His adoptive parents gave him a good life. Although the mother died, the father and I are great friends. He is grateful for the gift I gave him and I am grateful for the gift he gave to my son.

Unlike the Other Brother, his sister and brother were happy to know him and love him. He knows his family and they love and embrace him.

I am back in my heart at home and the circle is complete.

I can imagine how the Father of the *Prodigal Son* felt when he embraced his son for the first time. Although it does not say how long the son was gone, we can only imagine that it was probably at least a year or more; however, it does not matter. The loss of or separation from a child is a tremendously painful experience. As a minister, I have had to comfort and counsel many people who had lost a child. Many say you never get over it. I believe that is true.

That is the way God looks for our return—every moment of every day throughout our lifetime, God waits and watches for our return and when we are close by, the Robe, Slippers, Ring and Feast are made ready for our welcome.

We have completed this long journey from separation to unification—from loss to gain—and now we expect to be able to sit back, prop up our feet and take it easy for the rest of our lives.

It would definitely seem appropriate for us to expect that or at least an end to our challenges.

Unfortunately, or should I say fortunately, the journey is not over in the sense of the life journey. That phase of our journey is complete, making way for another journey. We have had many journeys in our lives; for example, from infancy to teenager, from teen to adult, from single to married, from married to divorced, from life to death. These are all journeys that begin and end, making way for the next journey.

And why was the Journey so long in the first place?

Truth be told, we are never really finished with our Journey even following so-called death. You see, the Journey is that of the Soul and not the body. While the body's journey is complete at death, the Soul continues its journey as part of its ongoing work of evolution. As it desires to know itself in more ways, it chooses another journey through the body in order to have the experiences it requires for the level of evolution it seeks. Each journey has its own goals and comes packaged with experiences that lead to achieving those goals. Depending upon what the Soul has chosen, it may be a life of quiet contemplation fulfilled through the vocation of a monk or nun or filled with great challenges that build and strengthen. The Journey is never meant to harm or to hinder; however, it may be perceived that way. It is a journey designed by the Soul to bring it closer to an awareness of all that it is and can be. It is a journey of the Soul, by the Soul and for the Soul.

Sometimes, like my daughter, we get a second life while in the same body; something dramatic or traumatic occurs in our lives that changes us at depth and we have a major shift in consciousness—an Awakening Point. In fact, I believe most of us do. There are some who may merely meander through this particular journey blissfully ignorant, as their Souls have so-chosen, but most of us do awaken. As such, the next part of our journey is a second life—a second chance to live in awareness of who we are, whose we are and how powerful we truly are.

The Journey was never about the destination; it was always about the experiences we had and the discoveries we made along the way. The real value of the Journey lies between the beginning and the end, that space where awakening occurred and awareness began.

Is the Journey actually long? No, not really. It is only as long as the distance between the head and the heart, which is based on how long it takes us to cover that 18 inch distance. The moment we realize we never left home and could not possibly be separate from God, the distance disappears, the body disappears and the conditions of love are met.

There was probably a motivation for leaving home long before the thought actually occurred to The Prodigal Son. Perhaps, early in life, he began to look around at his Father's great business acumen, his Brother's ability to fall right in and not only understand what the Father wanted but knew exactly how to carry it out. He probably saw how well they worked together and there may have even been some criticism from both that caused him to believe that somehow he just didn't measure up and could never be as good as they were. He would then have developed a Core Negative Belief that he wasn't good enough and set out to prove them wrong in order to be accepted and respected by them.

So, what's next?

To take the full process of the Prodigal Son's journey, the 7 Steps, as our own. Use them to pave the way for our personal journey. Study each step one at a time, reflecting journaling and completing each step as an individual exercise. Keep a daily journal as a map of your progress. Don't rush the journey, but be fully present and aware of each stage.

7 Steps to Consciousness—The Path to Home:

1. Know Yourself—Discover who you are and where you fit in the Universe
2. Unhook Yourself—Learn how to live with conscious awareness in the world of Duality
3. Surrender Your Will—Release the ego's grasp upon your mind and align with the Greater Will
4. Accept Your Assignment—Determine your soul's purpose and begin living from it
5. Work for the Greater Good—Live in awareness of your relationship to others and the planet
6. Live the Law—Awaken the Divine Power within by intentionally working with Universal Law
7. Keep the Peace—Contribute consciously and creatively toward peace and harmony in the world

The journey is simple, although not easy; however, if we just put one foot in front of the other, before we know it, we'll be there. This is a spiritual journey, not an intellectual one. We can't try to solve it or figure it out like a math problem. In HeartMath it says, "Thoughts and feelings play a major role in everything we do. It is through these inner processes that we experience our happiness and peace of mind – or the worst day we've ever had."[59] Allow Spirit to guide you through the process in a divinely ordered flow.

Remember the purpose is not the destination; the purpose is the journey itself and being in the moment every step of the way allows the insights you are seeking to come effortlessly.

Finally, there is no right or wrong way to take this journey. Set your intention and just start moving. God is watching the horizon

---

[59] *The HeartMath Solution*, Doc Lew Childre & Howard Martin, Harper One, 2000.

to catch the very first glimpse of you and will run to greet you as soon as you are in view.

Have a great trip. Bon voyage.

A PRAYER FOR PROTECTION

The Light of God surrounds me;
the Love of God enfolds me;
the Power of God protects me;
the Presence of God watches over me.
Wherever I AM God is and all is well.
And so it is.

AN AFFIRMATION

I walk with God and my way is clear, steady and perfect.

STUDY QUESTIONS:

1. What would "happily ever after" look like for you? (Describe it in writing.)
2. From what you have taken away from our journey with the *Prodigal Son*, what would it take to make it possible? What might be preventing it from manifesting?
3. What are you willing to give in order to have it? What are you willing to give up in order to have it?
4. Are you able to see instances in your life where you perceive something or someone in a certain way that turned out to be erroneous? (Describe it in writing)
5. What feelings/emotions did you have following your original perception? What feelings/emotions arose later?
6. What Core Negative Beliefs may have created the original perception? Where did they come from? (Write about it.)
7. Are you willing to monitor your perceptions and release your criticisms, condemnations and judgments in order to live "happily ever after?"

X

GETTING INVOLVED

The Journey of the Prodigal Son has revealed many important concepts about who we are, why we are here and what we are here to do. In discovering our relationship with God, which leads to understanding our connection to each other and the planet itself, we arrive at a deeper realization of our responsibility as inhabitants and co-creators of our world and the world at large. When this realization occurs, we realize further that somehow in some way, it is up to us to play a role in making this a better place. Our return to home, and the love that awaited us there, has opened the way for a deeper love to emerge from within us and that love has opened the way for compassion.

The dictionary defines *compassion* as "sympathetic pity and concern for the sufferings or misfortunes of others." The word originates from the Ecclesiastical Latin word, *compati*, meaning "suffer with."

This does not mean that we must go hungry, be homeless, have a serious illness or lose everything in order to experience compassion for our brothers and sisters. It means that we must have the capacity to understand what they are going through and to offer them the best of what we have—compassion.

In my early years as a student of New Thought Christianity, we were taught that people are where they are by divine right of consciousness. Today, even the Pope and the Dalai Lama are telling us that, once we have prayed for the hungry, go out and feed them. In other words, as I heard someone say many years ago, "put feet to our prayers."

I attended my first Parliament of the World's Religions this year in Salt Lake City and was stunned by what one organization has done to promote peace and loving relationships between the world's religions by bringing over 9000 members of over 60 of the world's religions together under one roof. There was not one incident throughout the week and the feeling of love and appreciation was so strong, we wore it upon us like the beautiful homecoming robe of the Prodigal Son.

I knew I had to get involved. I've had a yearning for some type of worldwide movement toward forgiveness for some time; thus, the forming of Spirit Awakened World Forgiveness Ministry. Then, receiving the 2015 Forgiveness Champion Award from the Alliance for Worldwide Forgiveness, I knew it was a louder knocking at my heart.

My friend, Olivia Herriford, has gotten involved by creating Women Sharing Wisdom (WSWI), a Non-Profit Organization dedicated to developing leaders for personal, professional and social change through the wisdom and knowledge of professional and experienced women. Through their core values, WSWI inspires positive change in the lives, careers, and communities of women and youth within the United States and East Africa.

A woman in our church has gotten involved by sewing dresses for little girls in Africa. She collects fabrics from people who sew or she purchases fabric with her own money or with money contributed by friends. Over the past few years, she has sewn hundreds of dresses.

Bob Plath, who discovered that the way to peace on earth was through forgiveness, founded the Worldwide Forgiveness Alliance, pulled together key people in our world in supporting its efforts to encourage the United Nations to establish an official World Forgiveness Day and is now coordinating the development of curriculum for teaching the tools of forgiveness in schools and community programs. I have volunteered to take part in the curriculum design. Our beloved Bob Plath just made his transition; however, his dreams are becoming a reality.

People like Oprah Winfrey, Steve Jobs, Bill Gates and Warren Buffet have been supporting the building of schools, digging wells, supporting farming techniques and more in underdeveloped countries and impoverished areas within the United States.

You are probably asking: "But what can I do? I'm not Bill Gates. I'm not a celebrity." To that I would respond every one of us can do something, big or small, and in our own way to play in part in healing and helping our world. Perhaps the exercise below, which we use in the "7 Steps to Consciousness Workshop" will support you in determining how you might get involved.

We all have a dream somewhere deep down inside. We all have gifts, talents and skills that can be utilized for world healing and transformation. All it takes is the desire. Once we tap into the desire, the Universe works tirelessly on our behalf to support us in bringing it to fulfillment. If you are not sure what you can offer to the world, the exercise below will support you in opening the way for Divine Ideas to flow.

EXERCISE: Getting Involved

Get some paper or a notebook and a pen. You may even type it directly into your computer or tablet. Be prepared to spend some time on this, even beginning on one day and finishing several days later. Don't just rush through it. Take it seriously and spend whatever amount of time necessary to really determine "What is mine to do?"

1. Take a few moments to think about the world as you see it now. (Write from your thoughts and feelings about what you have seen or heard on the news or a television or news report. Get down on paper all the feelings and emotions that arise for you.)
2. Choose an issue of great concern to you. (You can always take on another issue later. Begin with one to avoid feeling overwhelmed.)
3. List 3 things you can do about it: (If more than 3 come up, list them all, review the list and then pick the 3 around which you feel the most energy.)
    *   One that can be done immediately
    *   One that can be accomplished within 6 months
    *   One that can be accomplished within 1 year

4. Take the first step. (Set a by-when date, make a to-do list, list any information or contacts you may need.
5. Enroll others in your project. (Think of friends, co-workers, neighbors, family members or church members who might get excited about it.)
6. Create a plan of action for the other two things you can do; including prayers, affirmations, vision statements and other spiritual tools.

Once you get this rolling, you'll be amazed at how it will take on an energy of its own and, before you know it, people will be eager to support you in making this happen.

If there is still some doubt, some hesitation, that arises from feeling that you are only one person and that there isn't much you can do, let this poem reassure you that One is the greatest power.

> I Am Only One, but I am One.
> I can't do everything,
> But I can do something;
> And what I can do,
> That, I ought to do;
> And what I ought to do,
> By the Grace of God,
> I Shall Do.[60]

"Give, and it will be given to you. A good measure, pressed down, shaken together and running over, will be poured into your lap. For with the measure you use, it will be measured to you."
~ Luke 6:38 NIV

---

[60] Edward Everett Hale, In *Bartlett's Familiar Quotations,* compiled by John Bartlett, 14th Edition, Little Brown & Co., 1968, p.717.

For further information about these organizations:

Olivia Herriford
Founder and Board President
Phone: 925.930.7131
womensharingwisdom.org

Parliament of the World's Religions
70 East Lake Street, Suite 205
Chicago, IL 60601
312.629.2990
www.parliamentofreligions.org

Worldwide Forgiveness Alliance
20 Sunnyside Avenue, Suite A-268
Mill Valley, CA 94941
415.261.1393
www.forgivenessalliance.org

XI

EPILOGUE

The Journey begins. . .

As the Journey of the *Prodigal Son* comes to an end, my Journey begins. . .

Perhaps this does not make sense. I'm not sure it totally makes sense to me; however, I know that the completion of this book is a beginning for me because I struggled throughout the writing of this book. What began as a paper submitted to fulfill the requirements of a course at Unity Village on the way to becoming a Licensed Unity Teacher in 1999 that elicited the comment "this should be a book" became one of the greatest struggles of my life.

I struggled between completing this book or the one that comes after it. Even when my Astrologer/Intuitive told me that astrologically and numerologically (is that a word?), this was the one that needed to be completed first, I struggled. . .

I struggled with my right to put out such an intricate analogy and exploration of one of the most popular, well-known, widely-quoted scriptures of all time, in the midst of a plethora of brilliant authors who appeared on the Best-Seller Lists and on Oprah's Super Soul Sunday.

I struggled with my addiction to Procrastination. I had to enroll others to be my Accountability Partners, because I knew that I would not disappoint them and would work hard to have a good report when they called to make me accountable. And, yet, I still procrastinated and still struggled.

I struggled with my impaired eyesight, as I could no longer read the books which had underlining and notes in the margins to be incorporated into this book as support and emphasis.

I struggled with my guilt about not taking the time I was putting into this book to spend with my 85-year-old Mother, who existed within the routines of an assisted living facility in another city as dementia began to take a greater and greater hold on her mind.

I struggled to keep my commitments, classwork, quarterly reports and papers required by the Field Licensing Program as I moved toward licensing and ordination as a Unity Minister.

I struggled with the constant clamor of opinions among the Community of Selves that lived in my Subconscious and Unconscious housing complex.

I struggled. . .

Yet, as I look back over my Journey through the evolution of this book and the struggle that ensued, I am more deeply empathetic with what must have been a very similar struggle within the *Prodigal Son* along his journey and it occurs to me that we were taking this Journey together, supporting each other in making our way Home. I finally understood that, in order to understand his struggle, I had to experience my own struggle.

What has also become patently clear is that we are always on a Journey and when one ends another begins.

And so my Journey begins. . .

I AM HERE ONLY TO BE
TRULY HELPFUL

I AM HERE TO REPRESENT GOD, WHO SENT ME

I DO NOT HAVE TO WORRY ABOUT WHAT
TO SAY OR WHAT TO DO BECAUSE GOD,
WHO SENT ME, WILL DIRECT ME

I AM CONTENT TO BE WHEREVER GOD WISHES,
KNOWING GOD GOES THERE WITH ME

I WILL BE HEALED AS I LET GOD
TEACH ME TO HEAL[61]

---

[61] *A Course in Miracles,* Foundation for Inner Peace, 1975, p29 (Text)

DEFINITIONS

Here are some definitions to help you understand what I mean when I use certain key terms. They may be very different from your experience of the term, but just go with the meaning here and perhaps it will open up some new avenues of understanding that lead to at least a basic agreement.

<u>ALL</u>: The sum total of the consciousness in the universe, including all "pure" consciousness as well as that contained in every particle of physical matter.

<u>CONSCIOUSNESS</u>: The sense of awareness, of knowing. The knowledge or realization of any idea, object or condition. The sum total of all ideas accumulated in and affecting man's present being. The composite of ideas, thoughts, emotions, sensation, and knowledge that makes up the conscious, subconscious, and superconscious phases of mind. It includes all that man is aware of – spirit, soul and body[62].

The sum total of all ideas accumulated in and affecting man's present being[63].

---

[62] *The Revealing Word*, Charles Fillmore, Unity School of Christianity, 1959.
[63] *Dynamics for Living*, Charles Fillmore, Unity School of Christianity, 1967.

Teilhard de Chardin uses the term consciousness in its widest sense to indicate every kind of psychism – from the most rudimentary forms of interior perception imaginable to the human phenomenon of reflective thought. The within of things.

Def: The quality or state of being aware of something within oneself; the state of being characterized by sensation, emotion, volition and thought; mind[64].

INVOLUTION: The starting point of every form is an idea; infolding; always precedes evolution; that which is involved in mind evolves through matter.[65]

All of God's works are created in Mind as perfect ideas; God creates the ideas that form the things. This is involution.[66]

Spirit gets lost in its own creation – moving from God – a forgetting (Robert Brumet)

EVOLUTION: The development achieved by man working under Spiritual Law; the unfolding in consciousness of that which God involved in man in the beginning; the unfolding of the Spirit of God into expression.[67]

Ideas are made into form and shape. The working out in manifestation of what Mind has involved. Whatever Mind commends to be brought forth will be brought forth by and through the law of evolution inherent in Being.[68]

---

[64] *Webster's New Collegiate Dictionary*

[65] *The Revealing Word*, Charles Fillmore, Unity School of Christianity, 1959.

[66] *Dynamics for Living*, Charles Fillmore, Unity School of Christianity, 1967.

[67] *The Revealing Word*, Charles Fillmore, Unity School of Christianity, 1959.

[68] *Dynamics for Living*, Charles Fillmore, Unity School of Christianity, 1967.

Unfolding of Potential; unfolding of Spirit back into itself; moving to God – a remembering. (Robert Brumet)

COSMOS: The universe as an embodiment of order and harmony (as opposed to chaos); a complete and harmonious system. (Teilhard de Chardin)

SPIRIT: God as the moving force in the universe; Principle as the breath of life in all creation; the principle of life; creative intelligence and life.[69]

God is Spirit, the Principle of creative life, the moving life, the moving force in the universe, the omnipotent, omnipresent essence from which all things proceed.[70]

[69] *The Revealing Word*, Charles Fillmore, Unity School of Christianity, 1959.
[70] *Dynamics for Living*, Charles Fillmore, Unity School of Christianity, 1967.

BIBLIOGRAPHY

Biblical References
Harper Study Bible, Revised Standard Version, Zondervan Bible Publishers, Grand Rapids, MI 1971.
Message: The Bible in Contemporary Language, Eugene H. Peterson's Colorado Springs, CO: Nay Press Publishing Group 1993-96, 2000-2002). [Bracketed references]

Definitions
Webster's New Collegiate Dictionary, unless otherwise noted.

Metaphysical Definitions
Metaphysical Bible Dictionary, Charles Fillmore, Unity Books, 1931.
The Revealing Word, Charles Fillmore, Unity Books,1959.

My Recommendations for More In-Depth Reading

I am a life-long student. Even in my teaching and writing, I am a student. Below is the smallest of lists of those works that have shaped my life and this book. I list them for your enjoyment and to perhaps elicit, some of the same questions I have had. Enjoy and be blessed!

Atom Smashing Power of Mind, Charles Fillmore
The Biology of Belief, Bruce Lipton
A Concentric Perspective, Eric Butterworth
Conscious Evolution, Barbara Marx Hubbard
Global Brain, Peter Russel
God Doesn't Have Bad Hair Days, Pam Grout
The Healing of America, Marianne Williamson
How to Know God, Deepak Chopra
How to Let God Help You, Myrtle Fillmore
Living as God, Raymond Stewart
The Phenomenon of Man, Teilhard de Chardin
A Return to Love, Marianne Williamson
Radical Forgiveness, Colin Tipping
Your Soul's Plan, Robert Schwartz

APPENDIX I

CONSCIOUS EVOLUTION:
A BLUE PRINT FOR DIVINE POTENTIAL AND
REINTEGRATION OF THE COLLECTIVE

It is amusing that in the Star Trek movies and television series the Borg is portrayed as evil and something to be feared. The concept of one mind, working together as a whole and removing the individual imprints that foster competitive and adversarial conflicts, is depicted as being something which we must never aspire to. To assimilate the loving and harmonious healing role of the co-creative and give up the destructive ego-driven mechanism of individual glory and grandeur is subliminally messengered to us through the characterization of these 24th Century alien life forms. What came to me instead is that this was obviously a 20th Century preventive tool by those who fear that accumulation of material substance and power is in imminent danger when spiritual integration is advanced.

Assimilation Must Precede Transformation

A Course In Miracles says that God's creations ". . .seek to share rather than to get; to extend rather than project. . .want to join with others out of their mutual awareness of abundance."[71] It is our innate desire to create with God a "collective" consciousness for the "revolution" to the undoing of the separation and the return to wholeness. Therefore, this conscious evolution is inevitable. The Borg says: "You will be assimilated." A Course In Miracles says: You will do the curriculum. "It is a required course. Only the time you take it is voluntary. Free will does not mean that you can establish the curriculum. It means only that you can elect what you want to take at a given time."[72]

From the Pre-Life period all matter has been in a constant state of return to wholeness. As one particle of matter sought another by which to form a cellular organism, the retained memory of it origins as "The Collective" has driven it to seek its creator. So, too, have we as the grandest collection of cells retained the cellular memory of our Creator and perpetuated the Prime Directive to achieve the At-One-Ment of Creator and creation.

Therefore, if we are to transform the collective consciousness and successfully attain the next level of evolution, we must be assimilated.

A Critical Threshold

We are poised on the brink of future or failure. On the one side is the realm of infinite possibilities; on the other, the swirling vortex of self-annihilation. Each is an opportunity precipitated by choice. Our voracious appetites for greater technological advances,

---

[71] A Course in Miracles, Foundation for Inner Peace, 1975, p. xii.
[72] Ibid. Introduction.

128

extreme wealth and power over another have brought us to a cataclysmic juncture in our individual and collective evolution. Moment-by-moment decisions tear apart the foundation of our very existence and bring us perilously close to the crack in the cosmic egg.

Where, then, are we headed?

Teilhard de Chardin's writings indicate that we are in the Divine Milieu, where the current critical mass is on the verge of evolving beyond itself and a new form of mind is coming into existence. Our present is blending with our future and the earth is in the process of finding its soul. Humanity carries the future of the world within itself. The collective thought energies of all of the experiences of evolution has converged and encircles the earth. This layer, the Noosphere, is the sum total of earth's collective culture and from it will evolve a new kind of being.

There is a growing trend toward spiritual communication. People of like consciousness are being drawn together as if to create a network of consciousness-raising energies to counteract the senseless and wanton urges to conquer the elements. The fear of being consumed by that which we fail to comprehend drives us away from a more facile direction toward harmonics. We are a people at war with what is most natural to our core tendencies.

We are in chaos!

Out of Chaos - Transition

The beauty of our predicament is that Chaos always precedes transition. As we read our newspapers and reflect upon the six-o'clock news, the illusion of war, disorder, murder, destruction, disasters, inhumanity and hate press in upon us. It is tempting to dwell upon the projections of race consciousness and sink into an abyss of hopelessness. The appearance is: No Way Out!

We are simply on the verge of transition. Our people are being propelled out of bondage and the Ego (or old system) is feeling threatened and is acting out its need to self-perpetuate.

Killing each other is the ego's way of smoke-screening the recognition that love, not hurt or revenge, is the objective. The Course says " . . . every attack is a cry for love." Our cellular memory is simply recalling the loving womb of its origin.

Teilhard believed that as we expand our awareness of the universe its proportions expand in accordance with our awareness and we are threatened by the enormity of it – the unknown of it – we fear that it will crush us.[73]

The Course teaches that we have built our whole insane belief system because we think we would be helpless in God's Presence, and we would save ourselves from God's love because we think it would crush us into nothingness.[74]

Every transition begins with an uprooting of the foundation of a belief system. What we have held to be true, and upon which we have based our very existence, forms our belief system. When we find that what we have believed no longer holds us together and that there is nothing left to stand upon, we begin fighting to maintain our balance. The floor drops out from under us and we find ourselves clawing to hold onto the walls of our sanity.

As the Noosphere becomes denser our belief system is in constant flux. The more closely we are in contact with universal thought, the more we realize that what we believe is not true.

John David Garcia says: "A belief is a state of mind in which someone imagines something to be true. In science there are no

---

[73] Class Notes from Video: <u>Conscious Evolution</u>.
[74] <u>A Course In Miracles</u>, p. 243, 4:1

beliefs but only probabilities of certain relationships holding under certain circumstances."[75]

In our current state of mind, we are perpetually confused about what we really believe. Are we being led by our intuitive nature to move toward the next stage of evolution into wholeness? Or are we being directed by information and technology being fed into our sense realm via a continuous loop of input? Is what we believe about ourselves based on the "knowing" that is buried deep within our DNA and calls us to our reserved place in the Kingdom of Heaven? Or is what we believe about ourselves based on what we are told we are by those who strive to minimize our creativity to sustain their thirst for power over the thinking of others.?

The key to moving through the chaos into the new beginning (new consciousness/new birth) is letting go and letting ourselves be guided. In other words, when the floor drops out allow ourselves to free-fall into the unknown where Knowledge resides. This is the Void.[76]

From the Void to Love: Creating An Opening

Brumet says the Void is an empty space between worlds where you experience a sense of flatness, emptiness; a letting go of what was but not yet being ready to step forward. Transition is when we are changed by the occurrence; the Void is when we are reborn into a new beginning. [77]

As our society is structured presently, the space between our current condition of chaos and evolution into the Super Beings referred to by Teilhard de Chardin and Barbara Marx Hubbard,

---

[75] *Creative Transformation*, John David Garcia, Noetic Press and Whitmore Publishing; reprinted by cogenesis.com

[76] *Finding Yourself in Transition*, Robert Brumet.

[77] Class Notes - Transitions: The Wilderness Experience; Robert Brumet; CEP Unity Village, MO

engenders fear. The very nature of "unknowing-ness" is averse to everything we are taught.

From childhood through adolescence into adulthood we are taught that the key to success is knowledge. So we strive to become more educated, to obtain more degrees, to study under Masters in their perspective fields so that we will know what we do not know. Not to know is considered a detriment to everything society sets up as achievement. Yet only in not knowing are we fully present to the possibilities. In not knowing we are able to trust the process. In not knowing the Void becomes a safe haven from which to build our spiritual powers and emerge victorious in the Will of God.

Harmonic Convergence: The New Peduncle

Teilhard says that once we reach that critical mass where our thought energies have nowhere to go our evolution will either culminate in "The Big Bang" or the flowering of the New Peduncle because "all that rises, converges." The *Noosphere* is collecting the dissemination of human thought energies which are rising, unifying and converging toward a harmonic cogenesis. A new level of consciousness or new state of being is in its gestation period and we are its parents. Where we direct our energies at this critical point in time determines the evolution of our future.

We have relegated our peace of mind to a dependence upon external forces which threaten to destroy us because we determine our self-worth and value to society by our socioeconomic accomplishments and material acquisitions. We are aware of what our technological advances have done to the environment, yet we resist giving up the belief in our need for these toxic possessions. We pray to a deity outside of ourselves which has no personal investment in providing for us in a manner which is in harmony with life. We teach our children that knowing the ways of the world is a necessary factor in using it for personal gain.

But we have the option of choosing to live in harmony with nature and with humankind. By using our quest for knowledge to discover our interconnectedness and the positive codependency of man and nature, we may tap into the *Noosphere* and join in thought with other awakened beings to create a new collective of loving thoughts and actions.

As more and more awaken to the collective consciousness, the condition of rising thought is transformed from its present self-centered pattern to a new archetype where "the good of the many outweigh the good of the few."[78]

If we are to survive the holocaust we have rendered against humankind by our own insensitivity to the needs of our brothers and sisters, we must change our mind about how we feel about each other. We must begin to think of ourselves as a part of the whole and the whole as part of us.

It is interesting to note that, since all evolution flows along an identical pattern – microcosm to macrocosm – the transformation in the human dynamic can begin with one thought and flow outward to the whole. Therefore, we have the power to create an optimistic outcome one thought at a time – affecting a harmonic convergence into a new peduncle.

To quote Charles Fillmore, co-founder of Unity: "There must be a change of mind by the people of the earth before the tremendous uplift to be wrought by atomic energy can become beneficial and permanent."[79]

---

[78] Quote of the character Mr. Spock in Star Trek, original series.
[79] Atom Smashing Power of Mind, Charles Fillmore, p. 17

Omega Culture: The New Phylum

As we emerge from the new peduncle a new phylum blossoms and from it what Fillmore calls the "ideal man" or the Christ prototype is birthed. Our journey from the beginning (Alpha) is complete and the end is born (Omega). A new culture is developed where the resulting organism is in alignment with Creative Principle and the separation between God and Man is undone. The prophecy of a return to the Garden of Eden is fulfilled.

Barbara Marx Hubbard believes we are headed toward the creation of a universal species – to a life in outer space. She compares our astronauts with the early amphibians and feels that beyond the year 2000 we will be building many worlds throughout the universe as "Earth-space species."[80]

I hope that our disregard for the condition of Gaia is not predicated upon the awareness that there are other worlds, other planets upon which to establish our communities. This would indicate a perception of earth and other planets as useable and disposable and would begin a trend of planet hopping for the rape and pillage of the natural resources for our own selfish consumption. Since the inception of space travel, a parlor comment among African Americans has been that "now white men will completely destroy the earth and move on to destroy another planet." God forbid that we have reached such a level of callousness!

Ideally, as we commence our life within the new phylum and begin to co-create with God, our consciousness will no longer operate from the same perspective as human-thinking beings but as Christ-realized beings whose At-One-Ment with all life makes it impossible to harm a living cell without harming ourselves. Life as we know it now will cease to exist. Technology will elevate from

---

[80] *The Future - Previews of Coming Attractions*, Barbara Marx Hubbard. First Foundation News. August 1995.

telecommunications and scientific advances to thought-based development. Energy used to power our existence will have its origin within the realm of consciousness. We will drive our own existence. Medical science will no longer be necessary because we will live within an awareness of our innate perfection as Gods.

We will no longer need to physically toil toward the realization of our dreams. Love will work for us and leave us free to Be.

Conclusion

Our task is clear yet appears somewhat daunting. We are at the most expansive level of thinking that has ever been achieved in the existence of humanity; however, reversing the effects of the successful achievement of newer, greater and more advanced technology towards the benefit of Mother Earth and her children – while providing outlets for this more complex brain sphere – presents a challenging predicament for our society.

Our "Prime Directive," to quote again from Star Trek, is to undo the Separation. The focus must be on the return to spiritual mechanisms for living – prayer, meditation, forgiveness and love. The key is honoring the whole above the self.

The formula for evolution lies within the parameters of the teachings of Love espoused by the Masters:

Jesus Christ: Love ye one another; Love your neighbor as yourself.

Teilhard de Chardin: Through love and within love we must search for our Self. Love joins us with that which is deepest in ourselves.

Charles Fillmore: Love is the pure essence of Being that binds together the whole human family – the power that joins and binds in divine harmony; the greatest harmonizing principle known to man.

A Course In Miracles: Awaking unto Christ is following the laws of love of your free will, and out of quiet recognition of the truth in them.

Sheila Gautreaux-Lee: Love is the only way out of the present into the Presence.

As a Cultural Creative, my Directive must come through the diligent practice of moving from the without to the within. It is essential that my daily regimen comprise the following steps toward drawing into the collective:

1. Praying from the viewpoint that my needs are the needs of the Whole.

2. Meditating upon the connection between me and every living cell within the universe.

3. Acknowledging and practicing the presence of God in every aspect of my life, my mind, my body and my spirit.

4. Forgiving myself and all my brothers and sisters for our crimes against the earth and each other.

5. Making the most important commandment, according to Jesus Christ, my creed – loving my neighbor (brother/sister) as myself.

6. Recognizing the foundation of Good in everything, regardless of the erroneous perception within my limited purview.

7. Being willing to hear and obey God's guidance within my life and demonstrating the examples that manifest as a result.

8. Understanding that every attack is a cry for love and responding from that premise.

9. Letting go of any investment in outcomes.

10. Being *in* the moment every waking moment of every day.

As I take my rightful place within the collective, I call upon The Christ of my Being to guide me to the right place at the right time to be of service to humankind in its evolution into Wholeness.

We are the Borg. We <u>must</u> be assimilated. Resistance is destruction.

Note: I am uncertain whether this paper fulfills the directive of the assignment. As I placed my fingers upon the keyboard in their correct position and began to look at the blank computer screen, the words seemed to take on a life of their own. I must confess that at times it appears that I may be cheating. You see, I never write my own papers. Need I say more?

APPENDIX II

"Invictus"

Out of the night that covers me,
Black as the pit from pole to pole,
I thank whatever gods may be
For my unconquerable soul.

In the fell clutch of circumstance
I have not winced nor cried aloud.
Under the budgeonings of chance
My head is bloody, but unbowed.

Beyond this place of wrath and tears
Looms but the Horror of the shade,
And yet the menace of the years
Find, and shall find me, unafraid

It matters not how strait the gate,
How charged with punishments the scroll,
I am the master of my fate:
I am the captain of my soul.

Printed in the United States
By Bookmasters